Animal Wisdom Tales

Suzanne Thibault

Four Paws
Publishing

Animal Wisdom Tales

Copyright © 2019 by Suzanne Thibault

All Rights Reserved

No part of this book may be reproduced or transmitted in any form or by any means, electronic or mechanical including photocopying or recording, without written permission from the author.

For more information about his book or the author, visit: www.suzannethibault.net

Four Paws Publishing
www.fourpawspublishing.net

(P) ISBN 978-1-7341721-0-2
(E) ISBN 978-1-7341721-1-9

Printed in the United States of America, First Printing 2019

Cover Photo: Angela Kindley Dennis
Cover Designer: Tramaine Lott
Editing: Norma Springsteen
Stock Photos by Pixabay
Formatting: Wild Seas Formatting

All scripture quotations are taken from the New International Version (NIV) of the bible.

Disclaimer: The information in this book is intended for informational and spiritual purposes, not as a substitute for veterinary or medical care. Always consult a health care professional if you have any health issues for yourself or your pet. The author will not be held liable for any advice, suggestions, wisdom, opinions or omissions in this book.

Bonus - Free Pet Communication Mini Course

You can learn to understand the language of animals in this free foundational mini-course. Discover three easy to implement techniques to begin recognizing your pet's communication and practice sending, receiving and understanding their messages.

Our pets are talking to us all the time in hopes that we will hear them. If you are willing to listen, you can develop a deeper relationship with your pet.

The Pet Communication 101 mini-course features four modules that will take less than one hour to complete. You can then put into practice what you learned to begin communicating with your pet, deepening your relationship and understanding the animal guidance your pet is providing to you.

Register now and begin learning the foundation of animal communication at:

https://suzanne-thibault-academy.thinkific.com/

Table of Contents

Dedication 1
Foreword 3
Animal Wisdom Tales Mission 5
Chapter One - Realizing Dr. Doolittle-ness 10
Chapter Two - From Fear to Freedom 16
Chapter Three - The Miracle of Animal Love 19
Chapter Four - Animal Spirituality 23
Chapter Five - Animals are Sentient Souls 26
Chapter Six - The Human/Animal Relationship 30
Chapter Seven - Master Teacher Odie 33
Chapter Eight - The Elephant Encounter 38
Chapter Nine - Animals as Teachers, Healers, Therapists and Companions 45
Chapter Ten - Animal Communication Unleashed 52
Chapter Eleven - Animal Guidance for Self-Care 56
Chapter Twelve - Animal Wisdom from Beloved Pets 61
Special Guest Dr. Tricia Working, Alabama 70
Special Guest Catherine Moody, California 92
Special Guest Crystal Connor, California 112
Chapter Thirteen - Animal Wisdom from Ranch Animals ... 151
Chapter Fourteen - Wisdom of the Wild 160
Special Guest Debera A. Butler, DVM 162
Chapter Fifteen - Animal Conservation 189
Chapter Sixteen - The Snow White Life 193
About the Author 198
Recommended Resources 201
In Gratitude 202

Dedication

This book is dedicated to all the animals of our beloved Earth of sea, land and sky, who give voice to the truth of our Creator's glorious love and support of all of life – and to those human beings who love and cherish animals. Endless gratitude to the Holy Spirit for guiding the creation of this book in service to humanity.

To all the animals who excitedly shared their wisdom for this book project: the teachers, the healers, the counselors, and companions – a heartfelt thank you for awakening the human soul! To the wild animals who so graciously gave their wisdom for the betterment of human beings, I thank you for caring for us! To the animal lovers who whole-heartedly supported the creation of this book with your kindness and encouragement, I thank you!

To my husband and daughter who have supported me in in everything I do, thank you for being my life companions and believing in me and my purpose. I love and appreciate you both! To my five animal family members – Odie, Abby, Lily, Jack, and Luna, who love me unconditionally, I am so grateful to share life with you. All the teaching and love you provide on a daily basis has taught me who I truly am inside – love. You are the lights that shine in my heart.

May the animal wisdom presented here inspire you to

open your heart and embrace all living beings as fellow sentient souls and our partners in life. For it is through coming together and human understanding that we will all bring positive change to this world.

"Animals are the truest expression of love, here to remind us that we are too."

Suzanne Thibault, Animal Communicator

Foreword

"Just ask the animals, and they will teach you. Ask the birds of the sky, and they will tell you. Speak to the earth, and it will instruct you. Let the fish in the sea speak to you. For they all know that this has come from the hand of the LORD. For the life of every living thing is in His hand, and the breath of every human being." Job 12:7-10 (NIV)

These Bible verses are the inspiration for this book. They show us that we may learn from the animals all the wisdom, power, and goodness that is the Holy Spirit. Animals are sentient souls partnering with us in life. They are the voice of the Holy Spirit, embodying His unconditional love.

"Love makes life possible."

Luna, Tuxedo Cat

Animal Wisdom Tales Mission

Giving Voice to the Animals of Earth

As I sat pondering my life's purpose as an Animal Communicator and Spiritual Life Coach, I said a silent prayer asking for guidance about how I might best serve people and animals. I had been talking to animals for years and journaling our conversations. In 2016, a calling began that I could feel in my heart. At first, I denied this calling, not understanding it was coming from Spirit. When you ignore your inner guidance it becomes louder and louder until you listen. I finally decided I needed to step into my calling with both feet forward, which began my journey into Animal Wisdom Tales.

I saw news stories about animals gone astray, showing up in strange places. The first story I saw was about a baby sea lion found in San Francisco hanging out in a cement stairwell along Ocean Beach. Police officers responded and the baby seal snuggled against them for warmth. I heard the loving whisper of Spirit say, "Ask the seal if he has a message."

The officers named this baby seal George Bison. I tuned in with animal communication, introducing myself to the seal and asked if he had a message. The baby seal said, "Everyone gets lost sometimes. It's up to all human beings to help others. Don't be afraid, people appreciate help. I appreciate the help I got from the officers who rescued me. I felt so lost and alone, scared, and cold. Humans rescued me, and I encourage you to help others, both animals and people, because we all need help sometimes."

I was amazed at the depth of this seal's message, his kindness, his wisdom. This first experience birthed Messages of the Wild. Whenever I noticed an interesting wayward animal story in the news, I would talk to that animal and they would share their wisdom. It was so magical! I simply collected those messages and shared them on my website and on Facebook.

One year later I was sitting at my day job daydreaming about animal communication and how wise animals are when I talk to them. An idea so big and bright beamed like a ray of sunshine into my mind. It was overflowing with love and grace. I knew it was not my own thoughts, but the Holy Spirit who said, "Animal Wisdom Tales." Joy filled my heart and I realized that my soul's purpose had just lit up like a neon sign. Those words did not really make sense to me, so I asked Spirit what they meant. Intuitively I saw a book and received, "Interview the animals." My heart overflowed with joy realizing I had a purpose to fulfill, and Animal Wisdom Tales was born.

Animal Wisdom Tales provides a voice to the animals of Earth. Through Animal Communication, all species of animals have voiced their messages of love for humanity through Suzanne. They share inspirational messages of love to assist human beings to better understand life.

The animal messages of love convey their hopes and

dreams for a shift in humanity's thinking about how we treat ourselves and others, including the animals, trees, plants, and the various ecosystems on Earth. They ask us to open our hearts, see the Spirit inside each living person, animal, plant, tree, mountain, water, and blade of grass. Animals wish to work in partnership with you to heal the waterways, the food supply, your mind, and heart. Animals ask us to care for the Earth and all living beings.

Animal Wisdom Tales Mission

To receive the wisdom of the animals and broadcast their messages to all humanity for greater understanding and awareness of unconditional love. To learn directly from the animals and nature about their hopes and dreams in order to gain a deeper understanding of our spiritual connection and to share the animal's perspectives with the world.

Animals ask us to:
- Respect all living beings as sentient souls with dreams, desires, emotions, and a destiny.
- Agree to honor animal's spirits, keep them safe, and communicate love.
- Understand and embrace animals as teachers with guidance that is assisting us in understanding our human experience.
- Believe it is the birthright of all animals, both companions and wild, to live freely in places that support their well-being.
- Take responsibility for Earth's current condition and work to bring about positive change.
- Work in harmony with animals to foster deep peace amongst all living beings.

- Choose to care for animals with humility, respect, trust, compassion, and unconditional love.
- Honor our interspecies relationships based upon mutual understanding, service, stewardship, cooperation, and love.
- Dedicate life to fulfilling the animal/human sacred bond of unconditional love in support of the evolution of all life.

In celebration of Animal Wisdom Tales, both pet companions and wild animals' messages of love will show you what the animals are doing to help mankind learn, heal, and grow through their unconditional love. May you enjoy the animal wisdom that comes from pets and wild animals to inspire your understanding of life.

"Open your heart and accept animals as your partners in life."

Romeo, Polish Bred Arab Horse

Chapter One - Realizing Dr. Doolittle-ness

Wiggles was a small, white, curly-haired mutt with a fluffy tail. She was my best friend as a child growing up in a highly dysfunctional family. Her loving animal guidance showed me that love makes all things possible because her love was bigger than my fear.

Let me take you back in time. I grew up in a household where I wasn't wanted or loved. I felt like an outcast in my own family, so alone. I knew I didn't fit in by the way my parents treated me. I was cared for on the outside but discarded on the inside. All I ever wanted as a child was to be loved and accepted, to be seen and heard, but instead I was ignored, abused, and rejected.

I wasn't completely without love – I knew my dog Wiggles loved me. She was always by my side, making me laugh as we played together. She would cuddle next to me on the couch and lick my hand. Her love was kind and so important to me. Growing up in a household without love, I had comfort in knowing that Wiggles loved me. She was my best friend.

At age eight my highly dysfunctional "parents" did the unthinkable – they left me home alone while they went on vacation to Tahiti for two weeks. This was very traumatic for me. It was not like the movie "Home Alone" where eight-year-old Kevin goes grocery shopping and orders pizza. I fell straight down into a pit of traumatic fear, feeling terrified, shocked, and ashamed. My small body shook with fear, so much so that I couldn't handle it, and I screamed out in pain. This is when I first heard Wiggles speak to me. She said, "Don't be afraid, you are not alone. I am here with you and I love you!" Somehow hearing her loving words lifted me up and out of that deep pit of fear. I looked at her in amazement and I gave her hug.

Wiggles love was bigger than my fear.

I do not believe I would have survived that trauma without Wiggles by my side. Being abandoned and rejected by my parents broke my heart into a million little pieces, but it also allowed me to experience, for the first time, the true unconditional love of an animal which healed my heart. Today, through the unconditional love of animals, I am a professional Animal Communicator supporting animal lovers to communicate effectively with their pet and shine the light on emotional pain for heart healing as you make peace with the past.

Animals who grace our lives are angels in disguise. Maybe you don't live with a pet now, but at some point in your life I imagine you have connected with an animal. Dogs and cats are the only living beings on Earth who love you more than you love yourself. Animals are our guiding light that shine brightly when we feel lost. All you have to do is focus on their love and it will change your life forever.

Dr. Doolittle was my favorite movie as a child. I must have watched it a hundred times, wishing I could talk to the animals just like Rex Harrison did. Little did I know about my soul purpose then. I had lots of animal friends as a child, from the smallest of roly poly bugs to hamsters, rats, lizards, turtles, fish, and dogs. I cherished these loving relationships, as this was truly the greatest love I received as a child. As I grew older, I drifted away from my animal friends because they didn't live long and always left me with heartache. As an adult, I did not understand my strong connection to animals that stemmed from childhood. I had deeply repressed the childhood memories.

One day in 2008 I was sitting on the couch meditating with my current dog Odie, a Dachshund Terrier mix, sleeping beside me. As an empath, I began feeling grief that overwhelmed me and tears ran down my cheeks. I intuitively saw pictures of puppy Odie being kicked in the chest every time he barked. His abuse brought tears to my eyes, and I grieved alongside Odie, helping him heal his pain. Like really does attract like as I realized he too had suffered with childhood abuse.

This was my re-entry into the world of animal communication with Odie's assistance. He shared his inner pain with me and my compassion and divine inner healing helped him to forgive and heal his wounds of the past. I remembered my own childhood pain, and realized I also needed to forgive and heal my abandonment wounds too. In this way Odie was my teacher, showing me what I was holding onto inside to shift. I had buried that deep inside me because as a child the pain was so deep I couldn't handle it. As an adult, I could handle it, and this began my personal inner healing journey.

My memories of Wiggles came flooding in. I remembered how I could communicate with animals as a child and was finally ready to embrace this ability as an adult. It happened in a natural, easy way. It was if my soul was saying, "Now is the time!" So, I began having regular conversations with Odie, who became my teacher of animal communication along with the Holy Spirit.

Odie and I share a special bond – that of teacher and student. His big heart agreed to have about a million problems for me to help him with so I could learn and teach other animal lovers how to support their pet. In this way he is really the worst dog ever. I have to constantly remind myself that he is teaching me something and not get upset with him. It truly is the most challenging pet relationship I've ever had. Knowing that it all comes from unconditional love is the gift.

Odie's antics have included both physical and behavioral issues. He has overcome many problems with the assistance of divine inner healing. Odie has had separation anxiety, which caused him to freak out every time we left the room; PTSD type symptoms of being on edge and jumping in fear at every noise; fear stemming from abuse as a puppy resulting in aggressive barking and behavior towards other people and animals; peeing in the house excessively, destroying walls, baseboards, an ottoman, a couch, a reclining chair, an air filter, and more – resulting in thousands of dollars in damage.

Most people would have surrendered Odie to a shelter because they couldn't handle all that destructive behavior. I believe you don't give up on someone you love. While I have never learned the 'why' for some of these issues, many problems have shown me how animal conversations and divine inner healing can completely shift an animal's behavior and health. I now share this wisdom with other animal lovers so they too can support their pet.

The Dr. Doolittle-ness I was experiencing certainly was not as wonderful as the movie. I have experienced firsthand the deep effects that abuse has on animals – it can be so devastatingly painful for them – as painful as our own human abuse experiences. I have embraced my Dr. Doolittle-ness completely because I do not want animals or people to suffer with emotional pain anymore. I am grateful for my true soul's calling in supporting animals and their family members. Love truly makes all things possible!

"Love heals fear."

Odie, Dachshund Terrier Mix

Chapter Two - From Fear to Freedom

My inner childhood fears were deeply repressed from my abandonment experience, resulting in feelings of anxiety and depression as an adult. For years I suffered with depression and fear, taking medication which did not help me feel better. I did not understand why I felt depressed because there was nothing I was aware of in my adult life to cause this. It felt like I was dying inside, so I did the only thing I knew how to do – pray. I said a simple prayer to Spirit, asking for help in overcoming my emotional pain. The fear and self-doubt I felt had me on my knees crying out for deliverance.

Two days after praying for help, I was walking through the Target parking lot to my car. I noticed something shiny on the ground and bent down to pick up a small medallion. There was a photo of Christ inside the medallion. I found Christ in the Target parking lot! My life then began to change for the better as I realized my prayer had been heard and answered.

So began my personal healing journey to find my inner truth. This was not an easy journey, more like a winding, bumpy road. As I followed divine guidance which I knew was helping me, I began encountering obstacles. Mental lies, confusion, grief, emotional pain, self-doubt, and feeling not good enough created deeper fear that made me want to give up on life. I struggled to learn to use my intuition and follow it, living in indecision, learning how to step over fear and into truth. It was not easy, but I trusted the divine support I was receiving to help me move forward,

As I began embracing my truth as an Animal Communicator and talking about it to others, I encountered physical and mental interference against me from an unseen source. I would cry out to Spirit for help, each time receiving His grace. Through these trials I learned about spiritual warfare and specific self-defense techniques to help protect myself. I now teach these spiritual tools to women to help them overcome personal suffering.

I asked Spirit why my life was so filled with spiritual struggle. Well you have probably heard before that what you experience in life creates empathy for others. Those experiences have helped me provide compassionate support to those in need. Soul Safari was born to support women with truth about how to connect with and hear Spirit's voice, work with divine inner healing, communicate effectively with your pet and find the determination within to confidently pursue your dreams. It is not easy to work through fear alone. Know that I am here to support you with an understanding, compassionate heart.

I hate to see people and animals struggle. I have

walked through the holy fire and emerged into the light of love. Today I support women and animals to overcome emotional pain through the love and healing power of the Holy Spirit for a happy, balanced life.

"Fear is only the energy of your mind."

George, Rabbit

Chapter Three - The Miracle of Animal Love

It was a bright, sunny day in October as I drove home from work for lunch. I did that each day to allow our pups to go outside for a potty break. While driving home my thoughts drifted to our three-month-old kitten Rory, an orange tabby who had just been diagnosed by our vet with Feline Infectious Peritonitis (FIP), a viral disease of kittens and older cats that is fatal. The news at the vet was devastating for us, as Rory was our first cat family member, a kitten who was so loving and kind.

As a kitten Rory had no fear. When he first arrived at our home, we installed a baby gate to keep him from the dogs. Rory was eager to meet the whole family so he jumped the gate and introduced himself fearlessly to everyone, including the dogs! He was so loving to all of us, cuddling and purring in our laps. But he never played like a normal kitten and he did not gain weight.

When that shocking news was delivered by the vet two days earlier with tears in her eyes, I believed healing with the Holy Spirit would be the answer for him. Those two days were spent doing just that, providing prophetic ministry healing with Spirit clearing away the virus. The

FIP virus was nasty, energetically snarling, and resisted healing. Through my intuition Spirit showed me that the virus had completely engulfed Rory's body. The FIP virus had lodged itself in his gut, where fluid was forming, causing his organs to fail. After extensive prayer, the virus was eliminated through deliverance.

As I drove home that day I thought about Rory and his healing journey. He greatly appreciated the healing work. I got home and entered the house, and my two dogs eagerly ran to greet me as they always did. As I walked down the hallway and into the kitchen, I saw Rory lying motionless in the middle of the floor. I walked over to him and he wasn't breathing. He was dead.

Tears flowed down my cheeks as heavy grief overtook me. Our beautiful Rory was gone. I fell downward into grief, my head spinning. I felt I had failed Rory with divine healing; my heart broke into a million pieces.

My good friend Joy Howard just happened to be off work that day – interesting how Spirit always has your back. I called her up, choking through tears, and told her what happened. She came to our home, providing love and support that helped me find inner peace. Joy's calming presence and loving words were a soothing balm to my grieving heart. I am grateful to have such a wonderful friend.

That night I attempted to speak with Rory using animal communication, but my heavy emotions clogged up the connection. I got frustrated and spiraling thoughts of not getting to know him better and failing him in his healing journey filled my mind. I prayed for Rory's forgiveness.

As an animal communicator I needed to talk with Rory and get some answers. A few days later when I was feeling calmer, I made the connection. Rory was elated to speak with me in Spirit. He explained that as a stray kitten he had contracted FIP in relationship to a past life as a wild cheetah where he had also died from this disease. He had carried this virus into his new life to heal it.

Further animal communication sessions with Rory revealed that he wanted to heal the FIP disease in his tabby lifetime. He said he was now free from that disease forever, delivered by the Holy Spirit. He did not survive because the disease had weakened his body too much to recover. Rory's gratitude poured into my heart for his healing so I could forgive myself for thinking I had failed him. In this way he was my teacher, as I realized that his healing was not my responsibility, so I needlessly blamed myself.

Little did I know that the day after Rory's passing, my adult daughter had begun looking online at purebred British Shorthair kittens from a breeder in Grass Valley. She told me about this and showed me pictures of two available kittens. I could see the breadcrumbs falling into place. My heart leapt with joy when I looked at one kitten's picture and intuitively saw Rory's face superimposed over it. The kitten was a female, lilac colored British Shorthair, with a price tag of $1,000.

Oh the irony – Rory was a sick stray and now she was a healthy purebred. This kitten felt like a miracle to heal our grieving hearts.

Lily now rules our household as queen of the castle.

Her love shines through into my heart and our connection is strong. I delight in her chubby cheeks and plump healthy body. She is one happy British Shorthair kitty with an independent yet calm personality. A true gift of love from Spirit.

The spiritual lessons I have learned through my own animal relationships have had a profound impact on my life. It is in this book that I will illustrate the divine wisdom of how animals are deeply connected to us through a strong spiritual bond. With intention, may you find your inner knowing of your animal companion's guidance for you and how they support your life, for that love runs deep. It is a love that cannot be denied, a bond so strong it never ends, connected at the soul level and Spirit aligned.

"Peace is an inside healing job."

Lily, British Shorthair

Chapter Four - Animal Spirituality

Animal spirituality is Spirit aligned unconditional love and compassion. Job 12:7-10 shows us that all living things are the work of Spirit. The animals, the birds, the Earth, have teachings for us about life. You can talk directly to them to learn that wisdom using animal communication, or you can simply observe animal behavior as guidance and apply it to your life. There are signs and wonders all around you that you can become aware of and reflect upon to better your life. When you open your mind and expand your perspective, you learn the wisdom, power, and goodness of Spirit, in whose hand is the soul of every living being.

Animals are messengers of Spirit.

You can see animals in action each and every day in their spiritual work. Animals provide us with clues and guidance for our personal life through understanding their unique instincts, personality traits, habitats, and symbolic meaning. In this way, we can learn by observing and listening to the teachings of animals, the birds of the sky, the Earth and the fish in the sea who share Spirit's loving wisdom with us.

If you enjoy gardening or walking outdoors, I'm sure you've encountered a Bee. When we look at the Bee, we see a hardworking insect that produces a sweet treat, honey. Bees symbolize sweetness and the power to sting to protect itself. They teach us to work hard, stand in our personal power, and be sweet hearted to others. Even their honeycomb, which is a hexagon shape, is like a heart, symbolizing the sweetness of love and life that human beings can find in their own hearts.

Dogs teach us to be loyal to family, guard our home, and take care of each other. Dogs who learn to follow you as pack leader are demonstrating how you can surrender your will to Spirit. They also teach us patience, tolerance, faith, and trust. Dogs encourage you to play, have fun and explore the great outdoors. They model and teach unconditional love.

Cats are amazing teachers in the art of relaxation and peacefulness, which is their very nature. A cat will inspire you to get curious and hunt down what you want in life. They ask you to see the magic all around you as they chase dust specs sparkling in the light of the sun. Cats inspire you to have the courage to embrace the spirit of adventure and enjoy the roller coaster of life.

Animals are your guardians and guides which help to lead your way in life as messengers of Spirit. Animals act as a mirror to your soul. They are our caretakers who help us connect with and embrace inner love, for it is Spirit's unconditional love they express so beautifully.

The Animal Kingdom is taking an active role in the lives

of all human beings, yet most people fail to realize it. It is easy to run around with blinders on when you are busy with everyday challenges. It is time to awaken to new perceptions in animal relationships with profound life-changing effects. You do not have to have an animal companion to have animal interactions. We are all surrounded by wild animals and insects, trees, plants, and flowers we can observe and learn from.

"There are no limits to love."

Ardy, Norfolk Terrier

Chapter Five -
Animals are Sentient Souls

Animals are sentient souls, meaning they are able to feel and perceive emotions, show awareness using their senses to smell, touch, taste, see, hear, and communicate. Merriam-Webster's definition of sentient: "responsive to or conscious of sense impressions, aware, finely sensitive in perception or feeling." Your bond with animals opens a gateway for your own healing, as both animals and human beings are sentient souls sharing feelings and emotions.

I revere animals for their wisdom and guidance as an integral part of Spirit's handiwork, regardless of their color, shape, or brain size. The smallest earthworm is essential to maintain soil nutrients where we grow our food. Pets know how you feel, and work to show you so you can change and grow. Wild animals uplift us with their simple majestic beauty. We live together in an ecosystem of divine love that supports all life.

Animals bring us back to understanding our roots of awareness of the unity of all, of treating animals and all living beings with love and respect. While modern society reveres knowledge over wisdom, you have the power to choose differently, to make a spiritual connection and embrace animals as fellow sentient souls.

In seeing animals as sentient, you open yourself up to the communication that exists between all species.

Emotions are feelings in motion. Both human beings and animals have a full range of feelings and emotions. Understanding your pet's emotions helps you to understand how they are feeling. Your pet knows how you are feeling too, as animals read the feelings of the heart. They will bring painful emotions out in themselves (such as fear) to grab your attention to help you see it inside yourself.

As you have walked along your life path, you have had experiences that have left an indelible mark, shaping who you are today. Painful experiences that are not processed on an emotional level can become trapped. As children, we are not equipped to handle the pain of certain life traumas, so we repress it inside and forget about it. This is what animals sense inside you and mirror back to you, things that you are probably not aware of. It is the unconscious wounding from childhood that animals can feel. I'd say that skill shows us animals are teachers, healers, and therapists!

Animals also carry their own emotional pain inside from their life experiences. The most common trauma that most animals face is abandonment by their mother, which occurs when they are taken away too young. Animals also experience abandonment when surrendered to shelters at any age. Put yourself in their paws – you live with a loving family for years and are suddenly taken to a shelter, left alone, wondering where your family has gone, heartbroken. That universal pain of abandonment is heart wrenching for them. Animals can also suffer from abuse trauma, developing PTSD symptoms that can include shaking in fear or jumping at loud noises. Like us, they hold onto those painful memories and it affects their behavior as an adult in ways we perceive as misbehavior.

All animal misbehavior is based in emotional pain.

Every animal you have ever rescued, has actually rescued you. When we adopted Odie, I was not aware he was abused, abandoned and fearful, but he sensed that inside me and we made a heart to heart connection. It was as if we were made for each other; he knew he could help me. More importantly, it was Spirit connecting us, seeing how Odie would mirror my inner pain through his behavior which would help in my healing.

What I found in discovering that Odie and I shared the pain of abandonment meant that as I did my own personal healing work, Odie healed too. I learned how to facilitate divine healing of PTSD, leading Odie through a forgiveness exercise and watched his aggressive behavior shift into a peaceful demeanor. This is truly hands and paws healing together.

Dis-ease creates disease. Those unresolved inner wounds from childhood in both people and animals will linger, causing illness inside the body and emotional behaviors we find disruptive. If you are feeling down, you can seek help from a counselor or therapist. What do animals have? When we use animal communication to talk to an animal, we can help them heal their wounding, forgive, and shift their perspective. Animal communication bridges the gap between animals and humans so animals can heal their emotional pain. When animals heal their inner wounds, their behavior improves because they feel more peaceful and happier, and it is the same for human beings. This is the power of divine inner healing.

"See the loving connection we share together as sentient souls."

Mercedes, Papillon

Chapter Six - The Human/Animal Relationship

The close bond you feel with your pet is one of respect and love at the soul level. Many of us view our pets as our family members, understanding our pets' moods and personality. We love our fur kids and are always excited to talk about their antics and share photos on social media like the proud parents we are. The human/animal relationship is a mutually beneficial and dynamic relationship.

The emotional bond you share with animals has the benefit of increasing your awareness of love that is incomparable to anything else. There are moments when a single gaze into your pet's eyes communicates an unspoken language. It is a spiritual connection of love and caring reflected in your pet's behaviors. Animals understand the painful feelings we hold in our heart and through behavior show us what we need to look at inside. Think about your animal companion. No matter how neglectful you are of them, they still love you, no matter what. Animals model for us true unconditional love – the kind of higher love that Spirit provides us. They do not judge like we do but show us our inner patterns to heal.

This is a gift of love from animals, to surround us with their powerful love! The next time you are sitting on the couch, tune into their love and see if you can feel it around you, supporting you. Focus your awareness into your heart, notice your lungs breathing in and out, and have the intention to feel the love that surrounds you. Then give thanks to your pet for supporting your life.

This is the richness and depth of your relationship with animals. It is a beautiful expression of love. You share a relationship of guardianship and support for each other through love. Can you look into the eyes of your beloved pet and see their soul smiling at you? That bond of love is magnificent, there especially for you. Please do not take it for granted.

Animals can touch a part of your heart that expresses joy and the wonder of creation. This helps you to get to know yourself on a deeper level, helping you to reveal the truth of who you are, supporting you finding your spiritual direction. Animals teach you to how to love deeper, how to enjoy and appreciate being loved, how your love radiates out to others. Animals are teaching us the language of Spirit.

Animals can teach us to live outside of words, to listen to other forms of language, to tune into the rhythm of life. It is this rhythmic dance that provides you a greater understanding of life, entering into a state of deep connection with all of life. We can learn a lot from our fur kids.

You and your pet have a spiritual agreement with each other – to love, guard, guide, teach, heal, inspire, and walk together through life. It is a life partnership made in heaven!

"You hold the light of the world inside."

Piccolo, Cat

Chapter Seven - Master Teacher Odie

Growing up, animals were my constant companions whom I enjoyed hanging out and playing with. I saw my pets as my friends who truly cared about me. Never did I imagine that animals are teachers until I deepened my relationship with Odie. For many years I had a very dysfunctional relationship with Odie, judging his misbehavior, being frustrated with his barking.

It's easy to think of animals as jerks when they misbehave. I had to change my perspective and be willing to slow down and listen to him. If you grew up loving animals as companions, you may have never thought about your pet having feelings about things. When your dog destroys your favorite pair of shoes or your cat claws up the furniture it is easy to get frustrated. I've yelled many times at Odie for his antics, but it got me nowhere.

Odie is considered a Master Teacher in a spiritual sense. All of the 'problems' he has had have been for my personal benefit. That's a hard pill for me to swallow because the behaviors have been so frustrating. It has taken a lot of personal introspection to get to this point of seeing Odie's behavior as teaching and not get upset at his misbehaviors. In a way it has forced me to look inside and develop deeper compassion and understanding of how he feels.

Animals that are Master Teachers can exhibit challenging behaviors or health issues to help you embrace more patience, tolerance, compassion, empathy, forgiveness, and many other qualities. Your pet will keep acting out the misbehavior until you finally get a clue and make the decision to change. They are tenacious teachers in this way. It took me years, but I finally got "hit over the head" by Spirit, asking me to see my inner pain.

Each pet has their own unique soul purpose, so not all pets are Master Teachers. Pets mirror your emotional and physical issues to support your life, no matter their purpose. Master Teacher pets are more intense about it. For example, if you are stressed out all the time and irritable, your pet will mirror this by acting irritable. I have never understood why pets do this, so I asked Odie about it. Odie said, "Animals choose to help their family, and this is one way we do it – by being a mirror to your soul. When issues come into your awareness, you can choose to heal it and then the pet heals too."

I found this to be true of the relationship between Odie and me. For years now both of us have suffered with digestive problems with IBS type symptoms. I could see the correlation but did not understand what the situation was about. I was dismayed that Odie would take on IBS and suffer with symptoms – but also understood his teaching as a true example of unconditional love.

Animal Master Teachers hold divine wisdom and seem

to be able to handle any type of life trauma. They are powerful, Spirit-aligned old souls who have weathered the worst life has to offer in order to become the wisest of teachers in your life. When I was assisting Odie with healing his PTSD, Spirit would tell me step by step what to clear to restore balance. I have notes galore with instructions on healing every issue Odie has ever exhibited. Odie chose to do this for me to help bring healing to other pets, through their guardians learning Animal Communication and Divine Inner Healing for people and animals.

Animal teachers create spiritual continuity for human growth.

Master Teachers learn quickly and appear very wise in their learning. They will exhibit boundary, behavior, or health issues with consistency. For instance, a kitten might present you with boundary issues by nipping at your hands. This main issue will continue until both of you have learned. Then that issue will drift away, and another issue will pop up. This continues over and over with both of you learning and growing together. If you have a pet with consistent misbehaviors then you can assume they are a Master Teacher. The easiest way to find out if your pet is a Master Teacher is to ask them with animal communication.

Your own personal healing can be connected to your pets personal healing, as mine is with Odie. This means as you choose to heal your own wounds, your pet heals along with you. Your Master Teacher can even hold the same trauma as your own, mirroring life experiences which you heal together. As you choose to heal, you help your pet to heal too, hands and paws healing together.

If your pet is a Master Teacher, they will almost demand that you get on your personal healing path, in a loving way of course. Their misbehaviors will be ongoing, worsening if you avoid looking inside yourself. It is like your pet is saying, "Hey, get with the program!" In this insistent way they are helping you to learn and grow through for your health and wellbeing.

You can ask your pet with animal communication if they are a Master Teacher and be pleasantly surprised. Master Teachers choose to come to Earth to experience life in a body and heal wounds with their person. This is a healing partnership in action that a Master Teacher upholds to the highest level for your highest good. They take their job very seriously as guided by Spirit. Are you feeling brave enough to see what your pet is trying to tell you about yourself?

If your pet is a Master Teacher, get ready for a wild ride! Things will never be boring in your household and you will learn and grow together. Just remember that you are learning from your pet's misbehavior and let go of the frustration about their behavior. Odie taught me this, and I am forever grateful to him. I have literally changed from the inside out, letting go of fear, self-doubt, depression, anxiety, physical pain, and sadness, while learning to trust my intuition. Thank you, Odie, for being my spiritual teacher.

Odie, Master Teacher

"Your life is complete when you understand your relationship with the Holy Spirit. Animals help you accomplish this."

Chapter Eight - The Elephant Encounter

You can have relationships with wild animals. This came to light for me in 2017. It was a beautiful day in the northern California foothills. My friend Joy and I arrived at the Performing Animal Welfare Society's (PAWS) Ark 2000 Open House event ready to meet the wild animals. Little did I know that my heart would be captured by one of the animal residents.

We boarded a shuttle bus that drove guests to the various areas of the sanctuary, home to elephants, tigers, bears, primates, African lions, a black leopard, and other species. The docent spoke to us about the animals, their care, and their dramatic life stories. The animals there have come from captive environments where they were cruelly abused to perform or chained up in the back yard as 'pets.' My heart sank at these stories because wild animals belong in their natural habitat and no other place.

As the bus slowly rolled through the hillside, we heard the stories of the elephants who live there. We stopped at one enclosure and were able to get out to visit an elephant. Standing against the fence greeting us was a large Asian Bull Elephant named Nicholas.

Let me preface this by saying that when you are an animal communicator all animals can sense this and will freely talk to you. As I stood amongst the crowd of people, I gazed into Nicholas' eyes. I showed him my respect and told him how beautiful and magnificent he is. I intuitively began seeing images of his childhood in the circus where he was brutally beaten and forced to ride a tricycle. Tears rolled down my face as I felt his inner pain. I was wearing sunglasses so those standing around me had no idea what was going on. It felt like time stood still. As an empath I could feel his anger and hatred of humans.

I offered Nicholas Christ's assistance and asked him if he would be willing to forgive and help himself to heal. He thought about it and began expressing his pain. He butted his head against the gate as he released his childhood trauma (other people around me thought he wanted out). He then stepped back and sighed, and I saw his body relax. He then walked down the fence towards me, looked me straight in the eyes, and waved his trunk through the fence saying, "Thank you!" Tears rolled down my cheeks.

A Happy Elephant

Nicholas, Asian Bull Elephant

Just look at his smile! Nicholas continued to talk to me and said, "I ask you to volunteer here and help all the animals." I said to him, "I don't know how to do that." He then proudly posed, putting one foot up on the fence rail. He was showing me that he would handle it, all I had to do was show up and embrace my inner truth. I thanked him profusely for choosing to forgive and heal, for trusting me, and teaching me to be brave so animals can heal with the Holy Spirit.

I asked him his purpose in life, and he replied, "I am an Ambassador of Compassion." His life teaches us to hold compassion for all living beings and see them as kindred souls. In his kindness, he taught me that it truly is everyone's purpose to support animals, both our pets and the wild, with compassion and understanding. Thank you, Nicholas for choosing me to be an animal ambassador! May the compassion I hold inside for all living beings shine brightly in honor of you!

Nicholas' Animal Wisdom

The first Wild Wisdom Tale I'd like to share with you comes from Nicholas. Allow his magnificent wisdom to open your heart to new possibilities in life. His life story is one of redemption and resurrection through divine grace.

"Both people and animals are all creations of Spirit's love. Wild animals are not here on Earth to become your entertainment, pet, or enslaved to be used and abused or hunted. Throughout time, and even still today in certain areas, wild animals are enslaved into entertainment or service against their will, against Spirit's will. They are hunted for only the egoic power of human beings to feel superior to animals. They are chained up and caged up for your viewing pleasure, again against our will and Spirit's will. Do you really believe wild animals choose this life path to be your entertainment, captured from the wild, sold into captivity for you? No! Not one wild animal chooses this type of path.

"Let me share my life story with you to drive this point home. I was born into and enslaved in a circus, where as a young calf I was separated, tortured, beaten, threatened, and traumatized into learning to ride a tricycle for human entertainment. The trainer did not ask me if I wanted to do it, had no respect for me as a sentient soul, and looked at me as a commodity for making money. As a young bull I fell into deep depression, feeling isolated, so alone. I just wanted to be with my Mama. Deep fear of humans developed along with hatred, rage, and anger. These human beings I knew were evil to me. They did not realize how deeply they were wounding me, and they didn't care. They were motivated by the all mighty dollar and had zero compassion. They were oblivious! I learned it is easy for human beings to hurt others when they have no compassion or empathy. I sank inside myself to protect myself from them. I put up a wall around my heart to protect myself from their pain. With each moment of abuse my anger grew bigger and stronger. It became an inferno of rage inside of me fueled by the human predators' torture and abuse. I felt as if I had died inside and my spirit broke.

"As I got older, I grew bigger and so did my anger. That anger and rage could no longer be contained. It spilled out of me through my negative behavior towards them. I was bigger now and felt more powerful to protect myself, so I started fighting back. My behavior was telling them NO! Finally, those trainers could not handle me anymore and retired me. I literally said NO to them through my angry behavior, stood up for myself, and changed my life for the better.

"Suzanne's compassion and the love of Spirit allowed me to forgive those who hurt me so badly. She helped me to forgive and let go of that trauma. Her love showed me that there are good human beings who care. I have also experienced this with my caretakers at PAWS. The staff here take great care of me, they do have compassion and I believe they want a better life for me in the wild, even though I'm still fenced in. I accept I will never be truly free.

"It takes a community to care for everyone. To those who enslave wild animals – I forgive you and pray for your deliverance and judgement by the highest Source. For as a child of Spirit, I am set free from my pain now and have become an Ambassador of Compassion, spreading my unconditional love throughout the sanctuary and into the surrounding community and world. I am a beacon of compassion to light this world.

"The next time you visit a zoo, circus, sanctuary, shelter, pet store, amusement park with animals performers, or anywhere animals are held captive, enslaved or hunted in the wild, let my words inspire you to action of the highest love. Look into the eyes of those captured animals, let your compassion and respect shine brightly so they can experience it and know there are good human beings who care in this world. Let those animals know you respect, honor, cherish, and love them. Let your love for animals heal the wild animals in captivity for the highest good of this world.

"Please let your compassion lead the way and take action to help bring about change for any and all animals who suffer at the hands of humans. Rally to end animal performances and captivity. Speak up, share how you support animals, and take action. For it is only through the heart's compassion that we all may live together in harmony in alignment with love."

Nicholas, Ambassador of Compassion, residing at the Performing Animal Welfare Society's sanctuary in Northern California

Chapter Nine - Animals as Teachers, Healers, Therapists and Companions

The Animal Kingdom is filled with all manner of wise teachers, healers, therapists, and companions. Our pets support our lives, as do domesticated and wild animals. Animals partner with us in life if we are willing to be open to their teaching and counseling. When you respect an animal as a sentient being, then you can see their work in action and appreciate it.

Animals as Teachers

Pets who are teachers use their behavior to show you things to notice and change about yourself. Most animal teachings are related to your inner emotional state. Just becoming aware of this helps you notice when your pet is trying to get your attention.

Odie enjoys teaching my family patience when he goes out into the backyard to do his business. As a barker, he will stand and sniff the air, trying to find something to bark about. When we know he is done, we will call him to come inside. Odie will stand there, looking at us, nose in the air, and not budge. We will ask again, and he just stands there staring at us. Even if I thank him for teaching us patience, he still won't move. We usually close the door and walk away, unless he's barking, then we will go outside and escort him in. I wonder sometimes why Odie keeps teaching patience this way when my husband and I believe we are the most patient people on the planet!

Animal teachers provide behavioral experiences for your personal growth.

Most people assume their dog, cat, bird, bunny, or horse is just being obstinate when they don't behave as asked. Stop and consider what your pet's behavior might be teaching you. Animals display behavior for your personal growth. This is the teaching style of animals. Animals teach through behavior and body language.

Animals sense what you hold inside that no longer resonates for your life. Then they engage in behavior that reflects their lesson for you. Think about all the emotions that animals can express, and all the emotions you can experience. That is how far-reaching their teaching can be. They are considerate teachers, not pushing the limits of your trust, although that can happen to people who fail to notice the lesson and only see the misbehavior. When this happens, they blame the pet, think their pet is being a jerk, and get angry at them. That is not what animals want to happen though, so always look for the lesson behind the behavior for personal understanding.

Animals as Healers

Our dog Abby, a 12-pound Rat Terrier rescue, is a healer. Abby has been my personal teacher/healer, showing me what needs healing in my own life. She can sense my inner child and her behaviors show me what to heal. We have a true heart connection and I'm amazed at how much a tiny animal can express such deep love with confidence. She models so powerfully for me how to stand in my personal power with confidence.

Animals have the power to help us transform our lives. Their safe haven of unconditional love is a healing balm for the soul. We do not request their healing work but accept it as a gift when offered as it flows through Spirit. Abby will lay her paws upon the body and pray when guided by the Holy Spirit. Here she is in action for my husband's wrist tendonitis. She also counsels me to see a new perspective when I'm feeling down.

Abby the Healer

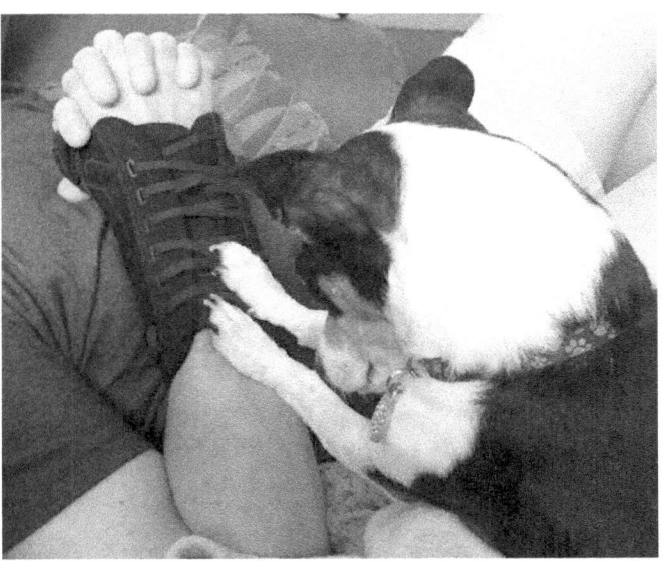

Abby, Rat Terrier Mix

Just as we human beings only facilitate our healing

work through Spirit, so do animal healers. You know when an animal is doing healing work for you by their behavior. Most animal healing work feels like you are having a hot flash, which is Spirit's holy fire.

Some animals will sit beside you or in your lap, some will lay paws upon you, some will walk circles around you, or lay far away from you. Each pet is unique in his or her healing work. All their healing work comes through their alignment with Spirit. They model this for us humans too who are anointed with divine healing. Animals provide healing based upon Spirit's guidance. There is a strange randomness to their healing that is much appreciated, especially when you realize that the Holy Spirit is actually behind the healing.

Animals as Therapists

Jack and Luna are brother and sister tabby cats, the youngest members of our family. They have taught me to not give up on things I want to accomplish and support my life in such unique ways. Luna acts more like a coach and Jack likes to give sage advice like a therapist. Both are counseling me in various aspects of my life. They appreciate that I am willing to listen to them and take it to heart.

Luna counsels my family by jumping up onto her cat tree every time someone walks by to demand petting. She is adamant about it. If we do not stop and pet her, she will jump down and follow us to grab our attention. Through this behavior she is counseling us to slow down and enjoy the small things in life.

Jack provides advice by laying on top of books I read.

I have a whole bunch of books only partially read because Jack says I learned what I needed and can move on. Jack taught me books are for knowledge and sometimes you don't need it all.

I trust all my animal family's teachings, healing and advice because Spirit speaks through animals. The wisdom they share with me sometimes surprises me at the depth of their advice. I wonder, "How did they know I needed to hear that?!" I realized that the Holy Spirit is actually guiding me through my animal's loving guidance, which can be easier to see and understand than using intuition. How amazing is that!

Animals as Companions

You can make a deep connection with any animal. All are our companions in this journey called life. Animals uplift our spirits, make us laugh and wonder at their beauty. Knowing I have so much support from my animal companions makes my relationships with them powerful for me. When negative behaviors occur, I ask myself what is being shown. This helps me to not get mad and to understand. Sometimes when emotions are involved it can be challenging to see the message animals provide with their misbehavior. That is when I rely on animal communication to talk about what is going on and work on a solution. It is about surrendering what you think is happening and take a broader viewpoint to understand what's happening through Spirit's guidance.

The most important thing I have learned from animals is that as teachers, healers, and therapists they love me unconditionally. This means that when animals speak or guide you, it is led by Spirit in their life for *your* wellbeing. They truly are angels on assignment, supporting our lives with love and guidance. This is the deepest relationship you can have with animals, if you are willing to open your heart, make the connection and appreciate their support they provide to you for your wellbeing.

Companions support you through petting, talking to, playing with, walking with, sitting with, and caring for them which strengthens your compassion and provides you stress relief. As your best friend they support your mood management, relaxation, distract you from negative thoughts, create physical activity to keep you moving, and provide social interaction so you never feel lonely. Pets companionship increases your positive feelings with their soothing presence. As a companion, your pet is a source of love, emotional connection, comfort, support, protection, and purpose. This is the power and purpose of pets.

"Animals support every area of your life as healers, teachers and counselors."

Daisy, Jack Russell - Chihuahua Mix

Chapter Ten - Animal Communication Unleashed

Animal communication transports you into the world of animals, their feelings, their emotions, their love. It is a beautiful form of communication that happens through the Holy Spirit. It is a language that bridges the communication gap between species as sentient souls of Spirit's love. Anyone can talk to animals, but are you willing to listen?

As animal guardians, we want animals to have a healthy, happy life with us. When you can communicate with your pet, you can know how they feel, where it hurts, and how you can support them, just like you do with your human family members. Animal communication empowers you in their care.

Every day the animals, both your animal companions and wild animals, are communicating with you. I invite you to open to new possibilities in living a life that is magical and miraculous with animal communication. It is a partnership based in love, communicated in love, and a true soul connection of love.

Animals are talking with us all the time, but we fail to slow down to listen. Human beings tend to walk through life with blinders on, not noticing the small stuff as we rush here and there. I invite you to open your heart to the wisdom animals want to share. When your dog excitedly greets you when you arrive home, he's saying, "Welcome home! I'm so glad to see you!" When your cat walks across your lap as you sit on the couch, they might be saying something like, "Time to take a break and pet me." When a hummingbird hovers near you they are saying, "Hello, I bring you joy!" Some animals are comedians and love cracking jokes. I once had a cat say, "Dog got your tongue?!" when I paused in conversation. When you talk to your animal companions, you get to know them better, and can appreciate their personalities and sense of humor.

Animal communication is a spiritual tool in alignment with the Holy Spirit. Spirit creates that connection between you and your pet, allowing you to use your intuition to have a conversation, you are not doing it yourself. It is a divine gift from Spirit to talk to animals, available to everyone with an open heart.

Animals truly love to talk! You learn about the experiences that have shaped who they are today. Most importantly, you can talk to your pet and find out how to help them with health or behavior issues. No more wasting money not knowing what's wrong with your pet. You can simply ask them what's wrong, they will tell you what the problem is and how they would like to handle it.

My friend Joy Howard has a dog named Andy. He developed heart worm and was suffering with heavy coughing and breathing difficulty. He had so many worms constricting his small heart it made it hard for him to function. Joy had me work with Andy to support his healing process. The vet had given two choices, one easy way and one harder way to medically heal the heart worm. The easy way involved less medication but had a higher risk of not healing. Joy decided to asked Andy what he wanted to do, showing her respect in his care. Andy and Joy agreed together to do the more intensive treatment of medication to get rid of the heart worm permanently.

Throughout his treatment I supported him with animal communication and divine healing. This assisted the medication to break apart the worms into tiny pieces for easy removal from the body. The danger was that the worm pieces could cause a stroke or even death. During this time Andy would tell Joy how he was feeling and tell her what he needed. He lost his appetite and told her why, helping Joy truly understand his needs. Andy made it through months and months of heavy medication treatment and is now free from heart worm. This is the power of animal communication and divine inner healing in pet care. What a beautiful relationship Joy and Andy share!

Animal communication also helps change behavior problems. Having a conversation around behavior issues is like being in a counseling session. You can ask your pet why they are behaving that way and find a solution to make everyone happy. You talk out the problem just like you would with a person. It is so powerful to have a conversation with your pet and learn how to help them so you can restore peace in your home.

Sometimes, the animal's behavior is directly connected to breed instinct. With animal communication you can ask an animal about their behavior and how it can be changed. They will tell you if it is a breed instinct they cannot control and offer up other solutions. It is problem solving in partnership with your pet.

Animals communicate through feelings. They speak through feelings, pictures, words, and thoughts that you then interpret with your intuition. Anyone can talk to animals if you have the desire to do so. It takes education and practice, but once you learn this skill it will change your life forever. You will create a deeper connection with your pet and all of life! You can learn to talk to the animals.

"Realize just how magical your life truly is and celebrate!"

Hannah, Shih Tzu

Chapter Eleven - Animal Guidance for Self-Care

Animals offer us the opportunity to reach our truest potential through a heart connection of love. Pets have an important role in our lives. Animals awaken and expand human awareness, love, and compassion. They open our heart to seeing and living life in a different way. Animals are helping us gain a better understanding of ourselves and the world around us.

As you glimpse life through the eyes of your beloved pet, you see the truth of who YOU really are.

Your connection with animals goes much deeper than you might realize. It is a soul to soul bond of love where communication is possible for a healthy, beautiful life. You can learn to understand your pet's guidance and how to apply it to your life, forging a profound partnership of hands and paws healing together.

Animal guidance is a form of animal communication you see through behavior and body language. With animal guidance, you use your awareness to notice pet behavior and then see if it applies to your life. It is about interpreting your pet's behaviors to see if what they are doing has anything to do with you. It takes an inner willingness to notice and apply animal guidance to your life.

The simplest form of animal guidance comes through your pet's unconditional love for you. When you walk in the door, your dog jumps for joy to see you, even if you were only gone five minutes. They are expressing their joy filled love for who you are. Your cat will come and lay next to you when you are feeling sick to provide comfort and companionship. Pets celebrate life with you, through all the ups and downs, with their unconditional love leading the way.

Animals can show us aspects of ourselves that need support and nurturing. This is one of the ways animals teach us about things in our own lives we can improve. If you are unsure why your animal is behaving a certain way, look at your own life. Could your animal buddy be showing you something for yourself or in your relationships with others that needs shifting? Animal guidance shows us there is something going on inside so you can get curious.

Your pet reflects to you that which you hold inside asking to be seen by you. If your animal is showing you unusual behaviors, observe the animal's actions, think about what you can learn from it, and take action for yourself. This is an easier form of communication from your pet who is acting as your life coach

My pup Abby was doing agility training to build her self-confidence. She is small and seemed to live in fear of many things. Agility training helps dogs build self-confidence by learning how to run through an obstacle course with you. For weeks I observed her approach the teeter-totter and stop, not getting on it, not moving forward, tail down, shaking in fear. The trainer said not to worry, some dogs are afraid of equipment. I relaxed, hoping the next week she would walk the teeter totter. Nope. Week after week she just stood there in fear. It took me three weeks to realize this was animal guidance! I asked myself how this behavior might apply to my life. I saw the sign of not moving forward out of fear, searched inside myself, discovering I wasn't moving forward on a project I had started. Once I realized Abby's animal guidance, I made changes in my business to work on and complete the project, and the next week Abby got on the teeter-totter with confidence and no fear. Truly amazing!

Animal guidance comes in many forms of behavior. One way cats tell us to slow down or take a break is by lying on your laptop or the book you are reading. If your cat stops sleeping in their favorite place, you can get curious – is their guidance suggesting you do something new or have you stopped doing something that you enjoyed? You look at the animal's behavior and reflect upon how it might apply to your life. It helps you to expand your awareness.

By observing your pet, you can improve your own self-care. If you can identify the issue in your life, you can work on changing it and then your pet's behavior will improve and so will your life.

Because you and your pet share a strong connection

of love, recognizing animal guidance is easier than you think. You know when your pet is happy, relaxed or not feeling well. Animal guidance messages are different, more subtle. You will see their messages easily and be able to look inside to understand if it applies to your life. You mentally scan through what is currently going on in your life and see if any animal guidance fits. Your pet senses something inside of you that you might not be aware of and you are working to bring that into your awareness.

Animals help you tap into a part of your heart that you might be unable to reach yourself.

Animal communication and guidance is a gift for your personal and spiritual growth. Be courageous and receive this gift from your pet. Animals are assisting you in life, offering a healing partnership for both of you. May you discover and embrace who you really are through your pet's loving guidance.

Here are three easy steps to begin noticing animal guidance:

- Observe your pet's subtle behaviors. Do you notice a repetitive behavior occurring?
- Look inside and ask yourself, "How might this behavior apply to my life?"
- If you see a connection, take their message to heart and choose to change.

Here is an example of how animal guidance works. I enrolled Abby in an agility training course to build her self-confidence. Agility training helps dogs build self-confidence by learning how to run through an obstacle course with you. For weeks I observed her approach the teeter-totter and stop, not getting on it, not moving forward, tail down, shaking in fear. It took me three weeks, but I finally asked myself, "What am I not moving forward on?" I realized I wasn't moving forward on a project I had started. Once I understood Abby's animal guidance, I made changes in my life to work on and complete the project, and the next week Abby got on the teeter-totter with confidence and no fear.

Animal guidance is a part of your deep relationship with animals. Pets help you restore a sense of normalcy and balance in your life. They are always by your side supporting you. Animals are there to make your life better. Your pet is fully supporting your life with animal guidance. All you have to do is notice.

"You can only help others if you are willing to take care of yourself first."

Gabby, Amazon Blue Front Parrot

Chapter Twelve - Animal Wisdom from Beloved Pets

Animal Wisdom Tales provides animal wisdom for greater human understanding of life and the world. Each animal interviewed for Animal Wisdom Tales was asked only one question: "What wisdom would you like to share with human beings to help us better understand life?" The animals I interviewed were so excited to talk! Each had so much to say, all expressed through their gigantic love for human beings. Each was thoughtful about what message they wanted to share that would make the biggest impact.

The animal wisdom shared here comes from unique animals with distinct personalities and life experiences. Their wisdom appears to come from their own life experiences with their family. Each is a beloved pet living with people who adore and appreciate their relationship. The wisdom they share is thought provoking, uplifting, and powerful. May you find inspiration from the loving wisdom these pets impart and allow it to change your perspective.

Intertwined are friends' providing special guest insights, personal stories and perspectives about their pet's messages and the relationship they share with their pet(s). Their heartfelt sentiments express their deep love and caring for animals as animal advocates.

A Message about Love

Andy, Norfolk Terrier
Joy Howard, Mississippi

"You are human beings of pure love. Please understand you can open your heart even bigger to give and receive love. There are no limits to love. The unconditional love of animals is supporting your life in a tremendous way."

A Message about Self Understanding

Chuck, Parakeet
Joy Howard, Mississippi

"You are free to fly! You limit yourselves with your thoughts that keep you tied up. Break free from those thoughts that hold you back, step off the cliff and take flight! Your life matters!"

Messages about Relationships and Life

Jessy, Domestic Shorthair
Norma Springsteen, California

"This world is one of community. You might not realize that humans and animals are so tightly connected. Many of you look down upon animals as a lower species. I will surprise you when I tell you we animals are at a higher consciousness level than human beings. We embrace and emit unconditional love. You all are working on doing this. The way you can express unconditional love is to set aside your differences and judgments of others, including animals, and open your heart to the wonder of all that is life. Your life is precious, you are pure love, you can see yourself as love when you choose to. Don't let fear or self-judgment hold you back from seeing the truth of who you really are."

"Did you know that we animals are supporting your life in ways you don't notice? Please wake up and start noticing how we support you. If you have a pet at home you adore, watch what they do each day, their behaviors, their sounds, their moods, and ask yourself how you feel inside too. Animals mirror to you how you feel inside. This is how you can see our loving support. Just expand your awareness and see all animals as sentient beings of love who support your life in a really big way. It is in this way that you can make a deeper connection with your beloved pet. Thank you!"

A Message about Healing

Cisco, Miniature Poodle
The Lendrum Family, California

"You human beings sure are good at getting stuck in your stuff. Did you know there is an alternative way out of your stuff? When I say stuff, I mean those heavy, deep emotions or painful memories. The alternative way is sometimes easier than traditional – because you are healing from the inside outward. I am in a healing family, and we as healers support others to heal those wounds inside. You can make the choice to participate in alternative self-care, and you will find the magical way of healing things so you can feel much, much better inside and out. Don't get stuck in your stuff, seek out healing work and let your life change for the better."

Messages about Happiness and Inspiration

Piccolo, Cat
Tanya Lochner, South Africa

"The sun shines each day upon your life. That sunshine is a message to you that you can be happy with your life. The sun never changes, it always shines. Sometimes it might be covered up by clouds, mirroring how your life might feel. You might have cloudy days internally sometimes where you feel bad. But there is always a light on the other side, and that light comes from inside you. Just as the sun shines, so does the great love you hold inside that is your light for the world."

"Those rainy days. Some people get stuck in their stuff, their bad moods, their bad days, their bad situations. It can feel like you'll never get out of it, but I'm here to tell you that you will. Being stuck is only a moment in time. Everything is in constant movement, including the situations in your life. Something better is always on the horizon. All you have to do is believe, have faith and trust. Your life is important!"

Messages about Relationships and Self Love

Simba, West Highland Terrier
Judy Anderson, United States

"Relationships are the most important thing to have in your life. No one likes to be alone. Please work on having loving relationships with everyone in your family, including your pet. Family drama can be intense, but just remember my words – love is all that matters. At the end of the day, after all is said and done only love remains. Bring more love into your relationships by simply remembering that everyone is a human with feelings, dreams, and desires. Even if you disagree with them, they are still worthy of love."

"Self-love is so important. Do you find it hard to love yourself? It can be hard to give others love if you don't love yourself. It's time for you to look inside and feel the love you hold in your heart. It is always there, beating in rhythm of your heartbeat, shining brightly outward to others. Your love is waiting for you to find it there in your heart. Let go of fear and learn to love yourself, care for yourself, and empower yourself. Only you can choose to do this. Some people think it is too hard or scary. I say, "Just do it!" Love is the most powerful energy in all the Universe, and you can tap into it any time by stepping over fear."

Special Guest
Dr. Tricia Working, Alabama

Dr. Tricia Working is a friend and colleague whose love of all animals runs deep. She has a large tribe of animal family members who support her life. Tricia is a fellow Animal Communicator who has authored the book, *The Fur Agreements*. Her strong connection with animals is inspiring. Tricia shares her wisdom about her pet relationships and messages.

"I have been connected to the animal kingdom always, having had animals all my life. For much of my life I didn't have the language to share the understandings that the animals gave me. I knew on very deep levels of their wisdom and kindness and spirituality and of their healing.

"For a very long time the knowledge and understanding was held within me quietly in my spirit. I knew how much love we shared, that the animals shared my sorrows, that they bring me a peace I had never known. What I shared with the animals I never found with humanity.

"I have a large tribe of animal family members. Rhett Butler and Little Prince offered to act as representatives within my family animal tribe, as well as the dog and cat worlds.

"Little Prince magically appeared on my front porch one Sunday 10 years ago. No one in the area had ever seen him, yet he found his way to me. He had clearly been abused, yet he still had trust in and love for humanity.

"He became my partner, going wherever I went, becoming my copilot on many road trips. He created friends wherever we went. At a conference, he became a huge star, everyone wanting pictures with him and even waiters bringing him tasty bites of lobster, steak and rich desserts.

"Little Prince loved me deeply, but with a quiet love, seeking only to be near me, holding space for those who had a louder, more insistent need. His love was steady and constant. Losing him so unexpectedly tore at the foundation of my animal family and brought powerful spiritual lessons.

"Rhett Butler is one of my original Atlanta kitties with jet black fur as soft as velvet. There had been a deep bond between us from the beginning, but as with Prince, I was not always aware of the space he held for the animal family.

"I only knew that each time I lost Rhett through passing, I became deeply aware within the animal tribe and me of his loss. The losses were made harder because each time I had been unable to say goodbye. The first time I lost him, he was literally back within a day or so leaving me caught in both grief and wonder.

"Holding Rhett had a way of soothing any inner turmoil within me. He was able somehow to help keep the animal tribe in harmony, acting as comfort when someone was in distress. Being Siamese, he was always talking to me, taking the pulse of the animal tribe.

"The messages of Rhett Butter and Little Prince came not as a surprise, but validation of my spiritual understanding of the role of animals in our lives."

A Message about Health

Little Prince, Pomeranian

"I want to inspire all human beings to better understand your connection with your beloved pet. We are connected energetically. That means that when you get sick or feel upset, we feel it too, because we are connected energetically. Have you ever wondered why some people who have Diabetes, that their pet also gets it? It's because your pet is taking on your energy to try to help you heal. It isn't always the best situation, because you don't want to see your pet sick. However, if your pet becomes sick, they are mirroring to you something to notice and heal inside yourself. They become your cute little inspiration of healing. So, when you feel sick, or have a deeper health problem, think about your pet and how they are supporting you. Thank you."

Tricia says, "Prince's lesson about mirroring was a loving reminder for me to pay closer attention to what my animals demonstrate to me daily. I know there are always deeper messages than what I see on the surface.

"His message was also bittersweet in that we lost him shortly after delivering his message here. I am happy to report however, that Little Prince has since returned to us and I am so much more aware of what he mirrors to me. He has taken just recently to chewing on my pens, which I know from before is a signal for me to write."

A Message about Self Esteem

Rhett Butler, Siamese

"I'm noticing a lack of self-esteem in human beings. Do you know what a powerful being of love that you are? I think you forget that, because I see human beings upset, angry, fearful, instead of feeling more joyful and peaceful. I have a tip for all of you. When you feel upset, focus your attention on your breathing. Feel your lungs moving in and out, supporting your life. Feel your heart beating, that gives you life. You are the love you hold inside. You are beautiful just the way you are. Set aside your self-judgment and see yourself in a new way – the way of love."

Tricia responds, "Rhett Butler's message on love was so powerful because it reflects the work I do with The Fur Agreements and the importance of being love. Rhett has come back to me three times. Now in particular he operates as a guardian spiritually and in the physical, escorting me all over the house. I see visibly that he is protecting me, and I am always aware of his energy, especially at night when I dream, making sure to be by my side.

"If I had simply heard the messages of my boys, not knowing them, I would think, what sage advice. But, knowing these are from my own pets, I know that indeed, the animal kingdom acts as way showers for humanity if we are but willing to see and listen. My spiritual journey would not be complete without their support and guidance. I am better, wiser, and more loving because of my pets. I am in deep gratitude."

***

A Message about Fear

George, Domestic Rabbit
Susan Marie, California

"Hop to it! Yes, I'm being funny! I'm a bunny and we

are funny. So, you human beings think you are all that. But are you aware that you are actually hiding in fear from many things? If you can just look fear in the face you will see that it's not really anything to fear. Fear is an imagination of the mind. Your mind is just playing tricks on you. Even looking at fear can be scary, but when you are brave and look right at the fear you can almost laugh at how silly it really is. Facing your fear can be the biggest challenge in your life – but just think about something in the past you feared and were you injured at all? No, because the fear was just fearful thoughts about something, there was no real danger to your life. Your life is Divinely supported, protected, and held by unconditional love. There is no greater love in all the universes. Align yourself with love each day and let go of fear."

Messages about Heart Connection and Dreams

Calvin, Maine Coon Mix
The Wilke Family, California

"The connection you all have with animals is profound. You can feel this connection inside your heart. You know it comes from unconditional love, but are you embracing that unconditional love? Or do you hurry about your day, running around doing errands, and forget to focus into our love? It's always available to you. I just ask you all to slow down your lives and notice the deep and powerful love we animals have for you. This love surrounds you everywhere you are, you live inside this love and can feel it, and experience it as much as you want. When you are willing to slow down and feel our love, it changes your life drastically because you are then living in a way that is connection and awareness of who you really are – love."

"Do you hold a dream inside your heart that you wish could come true? Any dream that would make you happy? I'm here to say don't give up on your dreams, not matter what happens in life. Those dreams are the fire inside your soul, inside your heart, that helps you live your true purpose.

"Dreams are powerful in this way, and when you begin to doubt or give up on your dreams you are really giving up on yourself. So, it's important to always have hope and hang on tight to your dreams. They may not manifest exactly as you imagine, your dreams might manifest into something even better than you can imagine."

A Message about Travel

Minnie, Persian Smoke
Daria Hill, California

"The animal/human connection is a strong bond of love. Our love together is so strong that it can never, ever be broken. So, when you travel and leave your pet at home, know that you carry that bond of love where ever you go. You might miss your pet or worry about them. Your pet understands your travel, or even when you go to work each day. However, we never know all your travel plans. Might you consider telling us, your pets, where you are traveling to, what day you leave and what day you return. This is just a common courtesy you can provide to pets so we can understand better your plans and when to expect you home. Animals do understand days of the week and time, so you can be specific. We get excited when we see you are excited to travel. Yes, we do miss you, but most animals are happier for you and don't get overwhelmed by fear. There are some pets who have fear of separation that might get upset, but you would know that and can deal with it. Also know that pets can heal separation anxiety; it usually stems from being taken from their mother too soon. Please, please, please respect your pet and talk to them as a family member would about your travel plans. That love will see you through to your return home."

A Message about Playfulness

Luce, Short-haired Tabby
The Estanol Family, Colorado

"Life is about being playful! Playfulness makes life more fun, more interesting, more exciting. Do you feel like you have a boring life? You can bring more playfulness into it by doing hobbies that you enjoy. What do you enjoy? Think about what you enjoyed as a child and do it now as an adult. There are so many things to enjoy in life, the possibilities are endless. Playfulness brings laughter, and laughter is healing on so many levels. The more you laugh and play the more you can truly enjoy life!"

A Message about Self Understanding

Romeo, Short-haired Tabby
The Estanol Family, Colorado

"Please begin caring more for one another. I ask all human beings to let go of judgment and see the truth of who people really are – love! When you care for others, you care for yourself too. Caring is sharing your love with others. What you put out into the world comes back to you tenfold. Animals show you their caring every single day. We ask you to share your caring with others too. It's easy to do when you set aside judgment. I encourage you to share your caring each day with only one person, and your world will change for the better!"

Messages about Compassion and Intention

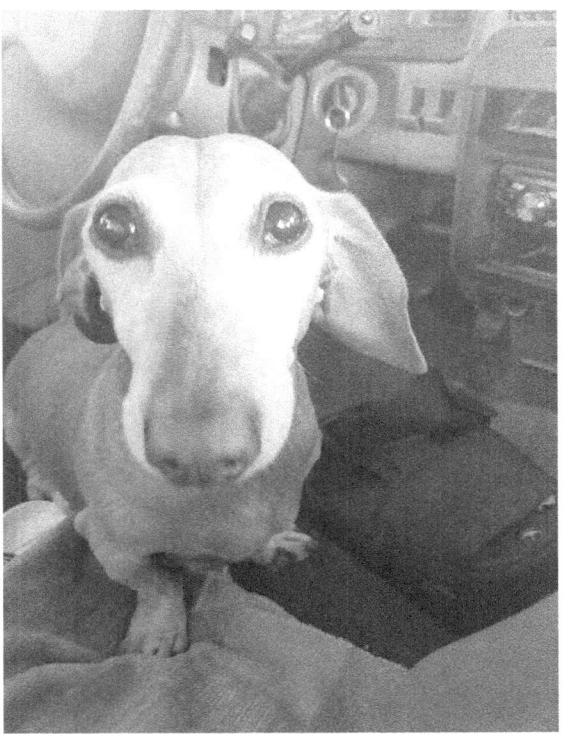

Moose Creelman, Mini Dachshund
Bernie and Chris Creelman, California

"Compassion. Every human being holds compassion inside their heart. Many of you may have closed it off, shut it down, so you don't feel it, but instead you feel pain. Compassion is necessary in life in order for everyone to get along with everybody. Compassion is based in love, given through love, felt through love, and when you allow your compassion to shine brightly to others it can change lives. Please open your heart to the compassion you hold inside and spread it around to others to make this world a better place for everyone."

"Help other people and animals for no reason. Do it with love, do it from love. When you give of yourself and help others it is life changing, because the person or animal that you help has great gratitude inside and you make them feel like you really do care about them. That's really all people and animals desire – is to feel loved, to feel needed, to feel important, to feel that someone does care, and know they are not alone. No one wants to be alone, including animals. We are all here to connect with each other through love. Please remember that love makes all things possible and allow love to lead your life and how you connect with other people and animals."

Messages about Energy and Feelings

Michael, Maine Coon
Bruce Feldhusen, Arizona

"You are surrounded by energies. You are beings made of energy. You can feel energy. I want to teach you all the importance of feelings. You know when you feel happy or sad, that is energy and you know how it feels. You can feel other energies around you. You can feel energies coming from other people. When you are having a good day, then talk to someone who is struggling, you might notice your energy being drained. That is an exchange of energy between you both. The person who doesn't feel good, is taking your energy to feel better. That is not a healthy exchange of energy. You don't have to share your energy in that way. The problem is only that you don't realize you do it, because it happens unconsciously. So, in hearing my message, you can become more aware of it and choose something else.

"You can choose how you want to feel and not take on other low-level energies that make you feel bad. It's only about choice! You have a life of inner power that comes through choice. So how do you not take on energy that feels yucky? You say no to it inside your mind, disconnect from it by visually cutting energy lines, and stating a personal boundary of protection. This will help you feel better!"

"You are a human being hard-wired with feelings and emotions. Many of you hide them because you don't want to feel them. It is normal and healthy to feel all your emotions that you hold inside. When you repress them inside, they can cause disease. I encourage you to look at your emotions first if you feel they are hard to experience. I'm talking about the negative emotions here. When you feel angry, upset, or frustrated, ask yourself "Why do I feel this way?" That is your first step in looking at the emotion. Once you become aware of why you feel how you feel, you can then make the choice to feel different. You can listen to uplifting music, you can have a cup of tea or coffee, you can redirect your mind into something more pleasurable. Nothing is as hard as it seems. All it takes is you being willing to use your gift of awareness and see what's going on in your life."

A Message about Perspective

Monet, Maine Coon
Bruce Feldhusen, Arizona

"Don't hold yourself back. Many people let fear or other thoughts hold them back on things they want to do in life. Animals do not have that issue because we live primarily through unconditional love.

"When you are able to look through the eyes of love, you look at life in a different way. When you hear those pesky thoughts nagging at you, just tell them to be quiet. Then make the choice to do something in alignment with what you want to achieve. Even if it's just taking baby steps you are still working on what you want and letting go of fear. This moves you forward in life."

A Message about Fun

Tom, Maine Coon
Bruce Feldhusen, Arizona

"Life is about living young at heart. Don't become weighed down by all the things in life that can drag down how you feel. You have a child-like wonder inside you that wants and needs to be expressed. So, have some fun! Play a game! Color! Do an outdoor sport you love! Think of what you enjoyed as a child and play it again! You are so much more than you realize inside. You might be good at hiding it but let me say it is safe for you to express your child-like goofiness to others. It's fun! Embrace your life through the eyes of child-like wonder and your life will change for the better."

A Message about Communication

Henri, Pomeranian Mix
Angela Dennis, Kentucky

"Do you realize that we animals are communicating with you all the time? We are so much more than just a pet or fur kid. We animals have feelings and emotions just like you do. It is my wisest wisdom to share with you and ask you to slow down, observe your pet, and see what they are telling you through their behavior and body language. Open your heart to our wisdom and your life will change for the better!"

A Message about Love

Kaylee, Black Mouth Cur Mix
Angela Dennis, Kentucky

"I'd like to talk to you about love. Animal's carry and model unconditional love for your benefit. We do not hold a grudge, although we can get upset or angry because we are sentient souls just like you. We live life through unconditional love, meaning that I love you no matter what. There is nothing that you can do to change this inside me. Even animals who are deeply abused by humans forgive and love unconditionally. This is the truth of the Holy Spirit's love, shared with you, through us. Embrace this love and share it!"

A Message about Messengers of Spirit

Freya, Cat
Angela Dennis, Kentucky

"Animals are messengers of Spirit. That's right, we work for the big guy! You think pets are simple animals with unique personalities. This is true, but we are so much more! All animals are highly connected to Spirit and choose to express Spirit's loving guidance. This means we are mirrors to your soul – your teachers, your healers, your counselors. All you must do is tune in and listen. Please expand your awareness, embrace us as your guides, and allow our loving guidance to support your life. You will be glad you did when you see how magical it is!"

Special Guest
Catherine Moody, California

Catherine Moody is a friend and fellow animal lover who adores animals and nature. She loves having adventures in the great outdoors with her two pups Skye and Hannah, the joy-filled dog sisters who light up her life. Catherine's Facebook community, Look What Beauty God Made, has a large following of nature lovers whom she inspires on a daily basis. Enjoy Catherine's heartwarming words on her pet relationships.

"Skye and Hannah, our Shih Tzus, are twin sisters born in the spring on March 1, 2008. They bring us joy every day, and never cease to amaze us with just how beautiful, thoughtful, and fun they are. While they are a little alike, they are really very different personalities from each other, and they are equally wonderful and loved. They are nearly inseparable and often snuggle with each other. We see them talking to each other all the time. They often chat about us silly humans and how to best deal with us, our requests, needs, and anxieties. They offer a fresh perspective from our own point of view.

"Hannah always wants to have fun. She is the most reluctant to leash up, and once outside, she wants to walk the furthest, explore new areas, see new routes, and just keep going! I love to walk, and explore too, a few miles each day, so Hannah is most like me in this way. Also, in the way that we both love to eat!

"Skye is the opposite. Although she is the first to run to the door to go out, she is always the first to want to go home. Skye wants to stay near and to return home quickly. Skye also is not food-motivated, more like my husband than me.

"Like Hannah, Skye celebrates life, but in her own unique way. She loves to flop and roll on the soft green grass whenever she finds the opportunity.

She stops and smells everything in her path and meanders on the leash. She is independent and insistent about whatever she wants. Although smaller of the two, Skye is very good at digging-in her heels.

"Hannah is always agreeable and easy-going, walks beautifully beside me, and will happily follow my lead, wherever we want to go. She patiently waits for Skye on our daily walks, wagging her tail, eager to move forward.

"While Skye is reluctant to meet people on walks, at home, and anyone who visits us, Hannah quickly agrees to being petted by total strangers. Hannah is brave when people visit, even if silently shaking while nearby. Skye will hide in another room until all other people have left. We appreciate each of them being themselves, and we do not attempt to urge them be any different.

"Hannah will always stay up waiting for the last person to go to bed before she will retire for the night. Skye goes to bed with the first person to sleep and quietly cuddles up next to them. Each night, Hannah stretches out, standing guard, on the foot of the bed closest to the bedroom door.

"The wisdom Skye and Hannah gave Suzanne were not surprising. They reflect what we have observed all along."

A Message of Life Celebration

Hannah, Shih Tzu

"Celebrate life! You human beings get so stuck in a rut, you slump around being down or depressed. Actually, let me tell you a little secret – you don't have to feel that way all the time – you can open your eyes, look at the sky, the trees, the flowers, the birds, your family, your friends, and as you gaze upon these beautiful beings you can realize just how magical your life truly is and then CELEBRATE LIFE!"

Catherine says, "Hannah said to *"Celebrate life!"* That is truly how she leads her life. She gets along with everyone in every situation. She looks for joy and happiness."

A Message about Fear

Skye, Shih Tzu

"Don't be afraid to live your life the way you want to live it. Do not let fear get in your way. Many people let that pesky fear inside run their lives. Well guess what? The fear that shows up is asking to be seen, heard, and let go of.

"It does not want to hang around, but if you ignore it, it will keep hanging around and bothering you. So, as the cool song goes, 'Let it go' and know that you are love inside."

Catherine responds, "Skye said to overcome your fears; and this reflects our own fears. Skye demonstrates fear to us daily, showing us how it inhibits the enjoyment of life. She often reacts to life with fear, and we continually try to reassure her that the sky is not falling, that she is very loved, and everything will be okay. Blessedly, when near her sister and surrounded in love, Skye is the happiest Shih Tzu on the planet!

"Hannah's advice to go outside and seek nature to nurture the soul is exactly how I feel. In 2012, I started a Facebook page, Look What Beauty God Made, to reflect this. This was long before I realized Hannah felt the same way. For years I worked in a stressful job that significantly impacted the lives of others with the choices I made each day. In going for walks every day with my camera, I learned to pause and see the beauty in nature all around us. It has brought me peace and happiness. I realized I needed to share this with others, to encourage them to go outside and look for the beauty all around, and to connect with creation. I hoped it would bring people peace and happiness too. This is exactly like my Hannah. Her spirit soars when she is outside with me, and her tail wags and wags the whole time. Hannah and Skye are both exquisite expressions of beauty and joy!

"Skye's words of dealing with fear reflect our own uncertainties. We do not know what life will bring and we fear our decisions that could lead to harm. We hold back from exciting new ventures, and glorious new ways that could bring great meaning to our lives. Instead of taking new opportunities, we see risks, and turn our heads, staying on the path we already know. Skye's advice is right on the money, and we would do well to heed her wisdom: *"Don't be afraid to live your life the way you want to live it."* I agree we should not let fear make our decisions -- fear seldom knows what is best. Skye says to acknowledge fear. I believe this means to see it as the liar it is, and then send it gently on its way. I find this hard to do with big things in life, the stuff that really matters. But I am learning to take the little risks, and as I do that, I find that new ways are not really that scary after all!

Hannah's and Skye's words are so supportive and so loving. It is overwhelming and wondrous to find out that our pets are here to support us. I observe them leading their own lives so selflessly and lovingly. I would be blessed to be more like Skye and Hannah."

***

A Message about Age

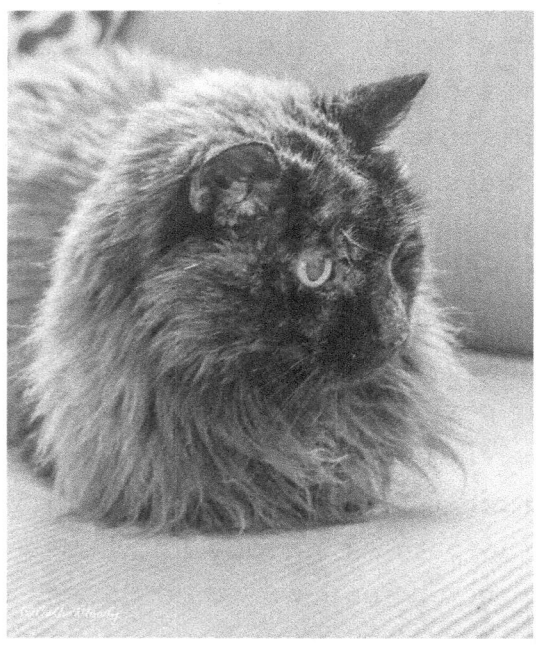

Twix, Long-Haired Mix (In spirit)
Marie Moody, California

"Don't let age hold you back from what you want to accomplish in life. Everyone ages every day! Age is just a number, not a life sentence. Yes, the body ages, but keep your mind sharp by playing games, gardening, staying active, even exercising and lifting weights. Eating healthy and exercise even help your brain feel younger. Age is only a matter of perspective. Get out and live life and let go of those silly societal messages about age. You are fantastic at any age!"

A Message about Emotional Connection

Pickles, Three Toed Box Turtle
Nancy Sandretto, California

"I'm a magnificent turtle. You human beings have preconceived notions about turtles, such as we are slow, and maybe not so smart. I'm here to tell you that all that silliness is not true. Turtles, as well as every animal on Earth, are sentient souls. We have feelings and emotions just like you do as human beings. We have good happy days and upset or sad days just like you. It is important for you to understand your emotional connection to animals, as we are helping you to open your heart to a deeper relationship with us, through our unconditional love. We share a deep hearted relationship that is a bond of love that can never be broken, even after passing we stay connected inside the heart. Please open your heart to your pet's or other animals love and emotions and understand and care for all the animals of Earth. Thank you!"

A Message about Decisions

Yogz, Nicolaus Mix
The Takayama Family, California

"Trust your instincts. Animals have instincts that help to guide our lives. So do you human beings, but most of you tend to ignore them. Your instincts do many things for your life. They protect you, they alert you to other people's feelings and emotions, they guide your way when you are willing to follow your gut instincts. Many people tend to over think things when trying to make decisions. I encourage you to look inside your heart, ask your heart what is the right decision for your life, then take action on that inner wisdom that comes forward. This makes life easier for you and you build self-trust in your instincts."

Messages about Love, Peace and Life

Songa, Siamese Tabby Mix
The Tiffany Family, California

"The truth of who you are is love. Love is all you are, love is in your heart to express outward and take inward from others. Life is truly only about love and nothing else! When you are having a bad day, you might not feel the love that you are. So, what you can do is to sit down and focus into your heart beating. As your heart beats, remind yourself of the powerful love you are."

"Everyone wants to feel peaceful inside. You have to deal with the busy mental chatter that can get in the way of feeling peaceful. So how do you quiet your mental chatter? You look right at what it's saying. Most of the time it is saying blah blah blah about stuff you don't even need to think about! When you hear that blah blah blah you can turn it off by saying, no thanks. Then focus your eyes and attention on something else more enjoyable."

"Life with pets is a gift. If you are a pet guardian (not an owner) then you love and care for animals. Know that your relationship is divinely guided and aligned. You are not together by chance. Your pet is helping you by supporting your life in many different ways. The biggest gift your pet gives you is unconditional love. You can tap into that love daily and experience a new way of living."

A Message about Life

George, Tabby
Kara O'Daniel, Missouri

"You can do anything you want in life. There is nothing holding you back but yourself, your thoughts and some of your feelings. It is important for you humans to learn that you are not the pain you hold inside or the pain you experience in life. Instead you are God's love inside, and that love and your pet's love are carrying you through life. Lean into that love, allow it to support you, and your life will change for the better."

A Message about Healing

Merlin, PomChi
The Allen Family, Oregon

"Believe in yourself. You are powerful because you are Divinely made from love. So many things seem to get in the way of living a happy life. Those things are there to help you look inside yourself and shift out of the struggle. We animals help you do this by showing you, mirroring to you, what you hold inside. We are very good at it! Animals support your life in a big way but you may not notice – watch us, observe your pet's behaviors and see if they correlate to anything you might be going through in life. Once you realize what you hold inside that is holding you back, you can heal it!"

Messages about Fearlessness and Wonder

Eddie Lewis, Domestic Shorthair (In spirit)
Kelli Russell, California

"Fearlessness. Have you ever faced your fears as a human being? Animals carry fear too for different reasons. It is easier for animals to overcome fear than it is for people. You all suffer with something called an ego, that pesky part of you holds onto fear like nothing else. So, when you want to overcome your fear, you really have to work hard at it and commit yourself to overcoming it.

I bet many of you try to stop or give up. You cannot overcome fear that way. If animals can overcome fear by facing their fear so can you! You are powerful inside! You are an amazing human being of love! You can do anything you choose to do! So, let me inspire you to overcome fear."

"You live in a world of wonder. Allow me to inspire your sense of wonder in this world. There are so many amazing things to see, to do, to read, to play, to feel, to embrace. Most human beings run around having a crazy life. All you need to do is slow down and smell the roses. Slow down and look around you – gaze at the sunshine, smell the wonderful smells of food cooking, listen to the raindrops on the roof, laugh at what you are reading. So many little wonders to behold. And when you look at and embrace those little wonders, your life becomes a great big wonderful life."

A Message about Connection

Chloe, Schnauzer-Yorkie Mix (Snorkie)
Jeanne Alford, California

"You are never alone! You might feel alone sometimes because human beings notice things like that. We animals can suffer from abandonment and feel alone and scared. If you have a pet you might notice your pet acting scared, and most of the time they might be afraid of abandonment. The way baby dogs and cats are handled we often suffer with abandonment because we are taken away from our mom to early. Sometimes people surrender their pet to the shelter, we animals see that as abandonment. I ask you human beings to open your heart to the animal's feelings and emotions. We feel as strongly as you about life, and abandonment breaks our heart. You are never alone if you have a pet because your pet is providing you with the greatest love of all."

A Message about Depression

Mickey, Maltese-Yorkie Mix (Morkie)
Jeanne Alford, California

"Do you ever feel down in the dumps or depressed? Life is meant to be enjoyed. I understand that life can be hard for human beings with all the ups and downs of life situations. Sometimes people get stuck down there though, and I'm here to tell you that you don't have to stay stuck. You can make a choice to feel differently. Does that sound hard? Well here's the secret sauce – your pet helps you uplift your mood. If you feel down, simply sit and look at or pet your pet, and watch how when you focus on your pet you shift your mindset. Isn't that a wonderful gift we animals provide? Now that you know and understand this gift is available, get petting!"

A Message about Companionship

Daisy, Jack Russell-Chihuahua Mix
Miriam Lancaster, Washington

"Companionship. An animal's love is unconditional and never ending. When you have a pet in your family, we are your family member, not a simple dog, cat, lizard, or fish that is a pet whom you can ignore all day. We are so much more than that. We animals are your companions through your life. We support your life in ways you do not realize. We are teacher, healers, and angels in support of every aspect of your life. As sentient souls just like you, we are helping to guide you and support you. All you have to do is open your heart and awareness to see our loving support. And by the way, as your companions, you are not our owners – you are our guardians."

A Message about Self Care

Gabby, Amazon Blue Front Parrot
Miriam Lancaster, Washington

"Hi I'm Gabby. You might think that Parrots are very

smart. Well, you are right! I want to talk to you today about self-care. Do you ever get so busy helping others that you forget to take care of yourself and your needs? You can only help others if you are willing to take care of yourself first. Find the love you hold inside and cherish who you are. Eat healthy foods your body loves. Sing songs that make you happy. Play games like you used to as a child. All of this is self-care. When you love yourself, you allow your love to expand outwards to others and they can feel it. So please, take care of others, but also take care of yourself. You are a precious human being of love. Take time to have fun!"

Special Guest
Crystal Connor, California

Crystal Connor is the biggest animal lover I know! She has nine animal family members, all rescues, all ages, whom she loves and cares for. Crystal believes in treating both people and animals with kindness, which is so easy for her because of her big heart. She is an animal advocate who champions the human and animal relationship. Enjoy Crystal's perspective on each of her pet's wisdom, which she shares after each message.

A Message about Spiritual Protection

Ashes, Great Pyrenees-Mastiff Mix

"Did you know that animals protect you on a spiritual level? Because we can read and sense energy, we know when something that is not healthy for you is hanging around needs to be cleared. Some animals are healers and can shift that energy for you. All you have to do is be aware and accepting of this gift of loving healing from your pet. You can also ask for Divine holy protection of your entire life."

Crystal replies, "It was so comforting to know that Ashes sees herself as my spirit protector dog and to find out we have shared many lives together. She had not been my dog initially. She came to me through a relative and a past relationship and it's a pleasure to be with her again. I feel so blessed. I have always had a great bond with her, and she is wonderful about trying to please me and be a source of strength, stability, and love for me. I see her looking at me and can feel the message coming through! Thank you, Ashes for your continued patience, gentleness, love and strength that you always exude!"

A Message about the Heart

Fluffy, Miniature Australian Shepherd

"Let's talk about the heart. Do you believe that your heart is only there to give you life? Well let me tell you that it is SO MUCH MORE than that! Your heart is actually your real mind, if that makes sense to your brainy mind. Your heart mind is where your truth is, where you connect with other people and animals. Where you feel your emotions and feelings. Your heart is more powerful than your brainy mind. Your brainy mind is important, but your heart mind is far more important, yet human beings tend to ignore the inner messages that come from the heart. That is your inner wisdom, your inner knowing of what is right for your life. The next time you need to make a decision, ask your heart, and see what it says compared to what your mind will say in fear. Your heart speaks through love, your brainy mind speaks through fear."

Crystal says, "I loved this message from my Fluffy and it couldn't have come at a better time to remind me what was important! I think he is totally on point that we as humans get wrapped up in responsibilities, stress, and fear/worry. Every time I read this message it takes me right back to center on what is important and gives me a great reminder of the perspective I need to be coming from when I try to solve issues and deal with people. I loved the reference about coming from the heart and asking your question to obtain it from a perspective of love which is what we are all essentially geared towards and lose track of in the hustle and bustle of life at times. Thank you my Fluffy for your kind teaching and wisdom!"

A Message about Perspective

Bruiser, Chihuahua

"There is nothing holding you back in life but yourself. You human beings are very good at letting those pesky thoughts, all based in fear, hold you back. You hesitate, you procrastinate, you doubt yourself. Oh boy. Just let that all go and know that you are a powerful human being of love. Love, love, love!"

Crystal responds, "I remember him saying love, love, love, over and over. He is so full of life and spice, love and joy! His message was a great reminder to not get stuck in my own head and doubt myself which I definitely do!

The other day I was sad and looked over and he was literally crying with me. He's such a sweet spunky boy and I love and appreciate him."

A Message about Self Esteem

Brittany, Chihuahua-Papillon

"Be the love that you are!"

Crystal says, "Little Brittany gave a short but very important message that really encompasses so much. Being love is who we truly are in our soul's essence and who we aspire to become despite what we go through in the world. Her message is a wonderful reminder that is our goal at the core of who we are is to be love, spread love, and that love with heal and uplift others along the way raising the love, joy and vibration of our planet."

A Message about Mental Chatter

Bella, Chihuahua-Miniature Pinscher

"The mental chatter that drives you nuts is only coming from fear. The mental chatter of fear is NOT who you are. You are the love inside your heart. The false ego or shadow side is there to show you what you need to shift inside of you. Animals can read and feel the energy of this false ego and your inner child. For example, if you are having a bad day, and feeling yucky inside with lots of negative talk in the mind, animals can read that, feel that, and then will act that out through behavior to show you and help you notice it, so you can shift out of it. Yes, it can be hard to shift out of negative thinking, but here is a tip. If you are really struggling with negative thoughts, and can't seem to shift out of it and feel better, then PET YOUR PET. The simple action of petting your pet, releases energy from your pet and their unconditional love to help you rewire that negative thinking into a more peaceful state. It actually, energetically shifts it out and provides you inner peace!"

Crystal says, "Bella's message is so true! I love that she is a teacher and can speak to the false ego which teaches us. It is comforting to see things from this perspective, that it is a learning experience in life rather than being hard on myself. Also, the realization that happiness is just a shift away. She talks to me with her barks and I definitely feel her telling me to get back on track and sending her love and wisdom with her feisty, loving, energy when I am imbalanced. Love my wise Bella."

A Message about Connection

Brooklyn, Miniature Pinscher

"You rescue animals for a reason. Deep inside your heart you know how important the animal/human connection is. How healing that connection is. How loving that connection is. You do not adopt an animal or rescue an animal by chance, it is all divinely designed. You are meant to be with the animals you are with, it is a soul destiny. Cherish the soul connection you hold with your pet or pets and live in their unconditional love every day."

Crystal responds, "Brooklyn's message was great confirmation about being meant to be with the pets that come into our lives and teaching for others who don't have any pets why having one in your life can be so amazing. She is so right about them providing unconditional love. Miss Brooklyn is very stubborn, going her own way, living her life dog that I know, but she also has a huge heart full of love for me. I love my Brooklyn."

A Message about Peace

Uno, Turtle

"Turtles are mainly about showing you peace. We are a very peaceful, quiet species. If you have a pet turtle, then you have brought a teacher into your home. A teacher of peace. All you have to do is watch your turtle and realize they are showing you by example, peace. Then you can bring that peace into yourself and feel more peaceful inside. Life truly is about love and peace. Search for your inner peace and discover a better life."

Crystal replies, "Uno came to me in a litter of orphaned turtle eggs. He was the lone survivor and first to hatch. He sometimes thinks he's a little like a dog since he's grown up around them and not turtles. He will swim so quick to complete for attention with the dogs! His conversation about peace is so true.

"Just being around him I feel his curious, sweet, inquisitive and loving nature. He is peaceful and takes his time swimming around. His gentle loving nature and wisdom have been a wonderful addition to my home, and I love him!"

A Message about Laughter

Cali, Cat Mix

"Laughter is what can help you feel better when you feel down. Laughter occurs not only for human beings, but animals too. We can make you laugh with our antics. You make us laugh with the silliness of your mental hijinks. It is so important to laugh, it is healing to laugh, it helps you feel better so do it often."

Crystal says, "Cali's message is a great one in that it reminds us play, laughter and fun are so truly important! They can be very healing and reduce stress while bringing joy into our lives. She is feisty, loving, and definitely playful! She will move her head downward and turn it almost upside down when she wants to play! Having her is a great reminder for me to play, and I love her!"

A Message about Feeling Alone

Chip, Cat Mix

"We animals can see when human beings feel lost in life. Many people walk around feeling alone, feeling lost like their life has no meaning. Your life has true meaning through God's love. Love is who you are, it is love that you can find inside yourself. When you find the love inside your heart, you connect with God and then you never feel alone. This is what stray animals do, they cry out for help from God and receive that powerful love that leads them to a better life with a family that adores them. You are never alone!"

Crystal responds, "Chip's message is so true and so wise! God loves us so much every day whether we realize it or not. I love that he brings up the topic of feeling lonely or disconnected from our infinite source of love which is God. So many people feel not good enough, have been hurt in relationships, or get caught up in the stress of life. His message is a great reminder that all we have to do is change our perspective and turn to God for help. That we are always loved and never alone! Chip was a stray feral cat who came into my life and is now part of the family and well loved!"

***

A Message of Hope

Oliver, Labrador
Rhonda Liebig, California

"Only you can change your life. You hold the power of love inside you. It is that power in alignment with Holy love that can lead your life in the right direction for your true purpose. Sure, you can muddle around in indecision and procrastination, but that gets you nowhere. Be brave, look inside yourself, and allow love to change your life and lead you to fulfilling all of your dreams."

A Message about Relationship

Teddy, Maltipoo
Maya Young and Teresa Campos, California

"The human/animal relationship runs deep. There is no deeper relationship you can have, unless it is the one you have with God. That is how powerful your relationship is with your pet. Do you listen to them? Your pet and all animals are talking to human beings. It is up to you to slow down and listen.

"We would appreciate it very much if you would listen because we have so much wisdom to share with you about your life. Your pet is either a teacher, a healer, or a counselor. Take a long gaze at your pet and wonder what they are and how they are supporting you in life. That is the power of the animal's unconditional love for human life."

A Message about Passing Over

Sinbad, Miniature Pincher (In spirit)
Marleece Peart, California

"When your pet passes over the rainbow bridge it can be very hard for you. I want to bring you good news! When an animal passes over it is a joy-filled experience. It is the same for human beings too! While those remaining in body are sad, those passing over are joy-filled as they have left a sick or elderly body that no longer functions and are set free into freedom, love, and happiness! Know that your pet loves you and can either return to you in your lifetime or will act as your guardian angel supporting your life. Let go of grief and guilt and connect with your pet's love in your heart."

A Message about Love

Bentley, Papillon
Kim and Becky Dove, Washington

"I am an animal of pure love. Some people cannot see inside an animal's heart. I would like to say to all of you, please see the love inside an animal's heart for it is unconditional in nature, and that means I do not judge human beings, I don't not get angry, no matter what you do in my life, I love you no matter what. The power of the unconditional love of animals extends through communities to anchor the energy of that love throughout the world. This is the gift animals bring to Earth, the entire Animal Kingdom is doing this. You can tap into your pet's unconditional love. Just sit down, focus on them, feel the love that emanates from their heart space. Anytime. If you are stressed out do it, if you are busy running around and need to slow down, do it. And know, it doesn't matter if you get angry at us; it doesn't matter if you yell at us; it doesn't' matter if you hate us for something we've done like chewing something up, or some of the behaviors that animals exhibit. it doesn't matter how you feel about us, we love you no matter what. There is nothing you can do that can break that unconditional love. You can break our hearts, for those of you who might want to hurt animals, you can break our hearts that way, but we always heal and forgive you. That is the power of an animal's unconditional love."

Messages about Animal Guidance

Mercedes, Papillon
Kim and Becky Dove, Washington

"The truth of who you are is love! The truth of who animals are is love! I ask all human beings to see the loving connection we share together as sentient souls. Human beings have feelings and emotions. Animals also have feelings and emotions just like you. Together we share those feelings and emotions as partners in life. I bet you didn't know that animals who are your pets are helping you to see things in your own life that you might want to change. We do this by being little mirrors for you. We are excellent actors in showing you through our behavior things to look at in your own life that need healing or shifting into a new mindset. This is the gift that we bring to you as teachers and healers. It is this gift that you can become aware of. When you become aware of the animal guidance that is going on inside your family you will be delighted! You will transform your life through your pet's loving guidance."

"I bet you are wondering how to see the guidance your pet is giving you! Most if it comes through our behaviors. Let's say you are walking your dog down the street. Your dog suddenly stops to sniff some grass, so you stop walking. You want to start walking again, but your dog keeps sniffing. So, you say, "Hurry up, let's go!" and your dog just stands there. What your dog is showing you is that you need to slow down in your own life and smell the roses. Slow down, take a look around you, and see the wonder that is life.

"Feel the sunshine on your skin, feel the breeze blowing through your hair, smell the smells of the great outdoors. This is what dogs do when they go for a walk, or when cats are hanging around outside. They savor every moment of life. You may think you are taking us for a walk, but in actuality we are walking you into a better life by helping you slow down."

"I know life can be hectic for human beings and pets can help you destress and slow down. Let's say you had a bad day at work, and you are sitting on the couch. If your dog is relaxed, they are showing you it's ok for you to relax too. Or maybe your dog greets you excitedly at the door when you come home, wagging his tail, jumping for joy. That is showing you how wonderful they think you are as a person. So many easy things for you to see if you will just be willing to use your awareness and look at them. The next time you see your pet exhibiting a behavior, ask yourself, "I wonder what my pet is trying to tell me." Then think about things going on in your own life and how the behavior you're seeing might apply to your own life. It's that simple! I wish you much success in this as you come to see your pet in a deeper way, building a deeper relationship."

A Message about Fun

Budrick (Buddy) Dove, Black Lab Mix
Rochelle Dove, Washington

"Fun, fun, fun, fun, FUN! You all need to have more fun in your life. You need to play more. I don't care if you are 90 years old, you still need to play and have fun. Whatever it is that you think is fun get out there and do it. Don't let things in life hold you back from having fun and enjoying life. Life is meant to be enjoyed to the fullest!"

A Message about Living Life

Mr. Miaou, American Shorthair
The Dove Family, Washington

"It's time for you to live the adventure that is your life. No more hiding behind the scenes. No more being scared. No more staying home instead of going out and having fun. It's time to embrace your life for what it is. Only you have the power to change your life – so take a stand for yourself, for your life, and begin doing the things that you love. Take baby steps if you have to. Just take action, no matter how small. Be brave enough to live the life God has given you and make changes if you don't like it very much. You are a powerful being of love!"

A Message About Desires

Leopold, Long Hair Chihuahua-Papillon Mix
The Dove Family, Washington

"You can do anything that you put your mind too. Your mind can also hold you back from doing anything you desire. Self-doubt gets in the way too much for human beings. Gently push all self-doubt aside, tell it you don't need it anymore. Then go out and do what your heart desires. Follow your heart it, will lead you in the right direction for what you want out of life. The heart's desires are stronger than doubt if you allow them to be. The choice is up to you. Silence the doubt and move forward on your heart's desires."

My Fab Five's Wisdom, plus One

Never would I have dreamed I would have five animal family members. Each one has their own unique personality, wisdom, and loe that they share with my family and me. All are rescues, except for Lily, although in her first life she was a rescue! I have never experienced this much love in my home, and it brings tears to my eyes to even think about how much furry animal support I receive each day.

I call my fur kids the Fab Five. They are my personal healers, teachers, guardians, counselors, and companions all with overflowing love. It is like Spirit, knowing my purpose, planned these four-legged connections of support to help me find my purpose. Our relationships have broadened my awareness of all of life, helped me to see what needed healing inside, and helped me to become who I truly am. I am excited to share their amazing wisdom with you, as Spirit is speaking! I thank Spirit for bringing these fur kids into my life. I may have had limited love as a child, but as an adult, love is overflowing in my home and I am grateful!

"Love Heals Fear"

Odie Dachshund Terrier Mix, Master Teacher

"Do not let fear run your life! I myself have experienced deep fear, but I always choose to shift it. I see human beings sitting in fear, afraid to even look at it. Did you know that when you look at fear you can shift out of it? Can you muster even a seed of courage to look at your fear? Or will you allow fear to run your life, making it a mess of unhappy feelings? The opposite of fear is love. Love heals fear. Which do you choose? I choose love and I hope you do too."

It is so obvious that Odie's life has the theme of fear. His puppy abuse set the stage for his life with me. He truly amazes me that he would choose this life of fear for my benefit, a huge sacrifice of love. I wonder at him as I gaze into his wise eyes, asking why he would go through so much pain just to help me. That level of unconditional love is almost incompressible to my human mind.

He was such a shy, quiet puppy who grew up into a big bundle of love. He is very vocal, making noises while playing, while being petted, while cuddling, so expressive and unusual. I asked him about this, and Odie said he likes to hear his voice – it grounds him into his body. We just ask him to be quiet, especially when watching a movie as it is hard to hear over his squeals. At age 10 he is starting to mellow out a little.

Odie has a good life with us. He has taught our family tolerance of the greatest magnitude imaginable. He has helped us to learn patience at a deeper level. Through this teaching, he has taught us about unconditional love. We love him no matter what he does. It is beautiful to see he has taught us so many things. Even though he still occasionally frustrates us, we appreciate his lessons very much.

Odie's job in our family is protector. He takes his job very seriously, barking loudly every time he hears someone at the front door. I cannot deter him from his job for it is his purpose within the family. We are sure his loud bark has deterred a burglar at least once. We appreciate his protection and his role in our family.

The message about fear Odie shares is a mirror to his own life experiences and a huge message for me. He models so perfectly how you can overcome even the deepest fears and find inner peace if you are brave enough to seek it. He has helped me to pursue my inner peace by teaching me to look fear in the face and heal it. Odie taught me to face my fears just as he has, and now we live in peace together.

One of Odie's most important teachings is an animal's emotional pain is the cause of all behavior issues. We can even say this holds true for human beings. This was a huge realization for me that transformed how I view life. Instead of looking at life through the eyes of fear and holding myself back, I can now see life through the eyes of love and pursue my dreams. I am forever grateful to one of the wisest teachers I have ever known – my soul buddy Odie.

"Change your perspective, change your life!"

Abby, Rat Terrier Mix, Master Teacher/Healer

"Don't take life so seriously! So many funny and goofy things happen every day. It all depends on your perspective. Are you aware you have the choice to see the positive or the negative in everything? You know, that glass half full thing? If you are having a bad day, pause, breathe, and ask yourself how you can look at the issue differently. Change your perspective, change your life!"

Abby is the light of my life. She brings me the greatest love and joy each day. As I gaze into her eyes, I see her love, can feel her love, and appreciate her love. She is my constant reminder that love is all that matters in this life, no matter what I go through. She cheers me up when I'm feeling down, cuddles right next to me hogging the bed, makes me laugh at her silly dancing. She is kind to others but holds her ground, not allowing the other animals to step over her boundaries. She constantly reminds me of her message to change my perspective, and sometimes that's challenging.

Puppy Abby meeting Odie for the first time.

Adopted as a rescue puppy Abby was so tiny. She

looked up to Odie like a big brother. She also learned all his bad habits, specifically barking. As she got older, she began standing in her own power and challenging Odie more for the alpha position, modeling to me how to stand in my own personal power. Today she is an assertive 12-pound pup with a big dog attitude.

Abby and I share the strongest soul connection of all my pet relationships. I adore her and cherish our connection. We have known each other through many lifetimes, sharing life's ups and downs together, always supporting each other. My life would be incomplete without her. Her antics bring me so much joy! Just gazing into her eyes each day fills me with joy.

I have supported Abby with divine healing of a past life she experienced as a horse. She told me in that lifetime she was BIG and powerful, and in this lifetime she felt so small and insignificant. She was learning contrast through these two lives and has learned to stand tall today by healing the wounds of her past.

The greatest gift Abby gives me is helping me see what needs healing for my inner child. She's taken to carrying around her 'baby,' a small teddy bear cat toy, in her mouth to show me my inner child needs nurturing. She guards that toy too, growling at the fur family if they get to close. This shows me my inner child seeks protection, which I ask Spirit to handle. She shows me through her behavior how to nurture myself.

Abby truly helps me to change my perspective all the time. I take her wisdom to heart, believing that when you do work to change your perspective on things, it does change your life for the better. Abby is a huge a gift in my life. Every time my inner critic pops up with lies, I simply look at Abby and soak in her love. I am forever bonded to my truest, dearest love of all – my soul mate Abby.

"Peace is an Inside Job"

Lily, British Shorthair, Master Teacher/Healer

"Peace is an inside job. Do you wish your life was more peaceful? The greatest gift of inner peace comes to you when you do personal healing work. As a healer myself, I can tell you that if you let those not so nice feelings fester inside, it creates chaos. Do not be afraid to look at your 'stuff' and heal it! How about letting Spirit have your back? Then you can relax and find that inner peace, for he truly is the Prince of Peace."

Oh, those cute chubby cheeks and beautiful golden eyes! Lily is the queen of our castle, ruler of all. She loves to perch up high, looking down upon all of us, observing the sometimes chaotic nature of our household. Lily epitomizes peacefulness, so her message is not surprising. She loves lounging in cardboard boxes, hunting bugs, and meditating.

Lily does have an unusual purpose in our family – it is her life's mission to bring peace and acceptance to Odie. Every day she attempts to lick him, snuggle next to him, play with him. Every day Odie denies her, grumbling his disagreement and walking away. They remind me of an old married couple. Lily is modeling the importance of never giving up on helping others. She is a healer who believes in Spirit's grace to heal the heart. Lily lives her life enjoying the magic and wonders of life. She loves watching light sparkles created by the sun inside our home, reminding me to notice the small wonders of life.

Gratitude from my heart to yours Lily, my peaceful soul warrior of love!

"A dream remains a dream without action upon it."

Jack, Tabby Cat, Counselor

"The dreams and desires you hold inside are the internal wisdom from your soul. It is your job in life to take action to bring those dreams and desires alive. A dream remains a dream without action upon it. When you take action, any action, it moves you forward in the right direction of fulfilling dreams. See yourself as already having your dreams fulfilled and it will become so. The power of the human imagination is vast, use it to your advantage and shut up the inner critic. Your dreams matter!"

Jack and Luna were found dumped with the rest of their littermates at my daughter's place of employment at about four weeks old. When they were brought into the office, it was love at first sight for the staff. My daughter excitedly called me asking if we would foster one of the kittens. My intuition said to bring two home to foster so they had company. So, home came Jack and Luna, tiny little kittens filled with love.

It was with the intention to foster these two until ready for adoption but something happened. My husband couldn't let go, so Jack and Luna became a part of our family. We could not give up "the babies" to another family. Odie and Lily did not like this though. They felt like their boundaries were threatened, and tensions arose. Time heals wounds and relationships. Today, Odie ignores them and Lily bosses them around.

Jack is a self-proclaimed adventurer and counselor. Once he realized I was an animal communicator he told me he was staying in our family. We have watched him grow from a tiny kitten to a big cat with lots of energy, so much so we got him a cat wheel which he runs on each night. He also loves lounging in boxes and hunting. He is easily bored and is the instigator of household disruption.

As a therapist, Jack truly understands my small business and provides advice. He is able to see my dreams and desires for a different life and encourages me forward. I could never give up on my business with Jack as my counselor. His wisdom to take action upon your dreams to bring them into reality speaks to my heart. Thank you, Jack, my mighty soul counselor!

"Love Makes Life Possible"

Luna, Tuxedo Cat, Counselor

Love makes life possible. Without Spirit's love, your life would suck! Love comes in many forms and is all around you, but the greatest love of all you hold inside your heart. That internal love is the holy love of our Creator. That love is so strong and powerful that it creates life for you. It is up to you to live the life you choose – love or fear. I hope you'll always choose love and seek out the love you hold inside on a deeper level."

Lovely Luna is my spiritual caretaker as a counselor. She is the gentlest of souls, providing loving counseling that feels as if Spirit is speaking directly to me. She is an excellent model of fearlessness, for she has chosen Spirit's love over fear. While I see our other pets jump in fear at noises, Luna is always calm and peaceful, a true testament to divine love.

Luna is the most magical of our cats. She is in many ways mystical in the way she interacts with us. She is the only fur kid who will not sit on our laps. She will lay next to us if there is a warm blanket to lounge on. I almost feel she's smarter than the rest of us since she exhibits such confidence in her relationship with Spirit, a confidence so deep it crowds out fear, allowing for deep inner peace. She is an excellent role model on how to live a life of peaceful divine alignment.

She also has this quirky desire to knock items off of the counter, end table, and even the walls. She has climbed up on the fireplace mantel, stood up with her front paws up on the wall, and knocked down a large, heavy framed picture, destroying it. Her behavior teaches us not to take life so seriously. Her message that love makes life possible is simple spiritual truth I take to heart. Much love to you Luna, my amazing soul guide!

"Appreciate all Animals"

Goldy, Goldfish (In spirit)

"Goldfish are gentle souls who emanate peace to you. You can talk to us anytime and we understand you. You can talk to any animal and they understand, for Spirit facilitates interspecies communication. You can learn to hear us too, for water does not block communication that comes from the heart. As you glide through the water of life, may you begin to appreciate all animals as your friends and supporters of your life."

We once had a goldfish named Goldy. She was so fun to talk to. I appreciate Goldy's message as a reminder to appreciate animals as sentient souls, to gaze into their eyes and see their love, even the tiny ones. She taught me that even the tiniest animals have a big heart. Thank you Goldy!

***

I hope these messages from beloved pets have inspired you to better understand your own pet(s), to see them as your teacher, your healer, your therapist, and companion as a messenger of Spirit. Your connection with your pet runs deeper than just companionship, it is two souls on a journey through life together. I hope you will begin exploring your pet relationship and get curious about what your pet is trying to tell you, for there is no greater delight than the love of an animal and understanding how much they support your life.

Chapter Thirteen - Animal Wisdom from Ranch Animals

The Ranch Animals wisdom shared here comes from people who have animals and my own encounters with ranch animals in my community. They are amazing souls in service to humanity in so many different ways. Their greatest gift is their loving wisdom.

A Message about Partnership

Romeo, Polish Bred Arab Horse (In Spirit)
Sandy J. Colling, California

"Animals are here on Earth to support human life. Many people do not realize this and look upon animals as a lower life form. Well guess what? We are not! We are actually much wiser than human beings because we embody unconditional love and you all struggle to do that. You human beings struggle with judgment, and expectations, and assumptions that are really all imaginary lies of the mind. Animals do not have a shadow side, so we act as your guardians, as your counselors in life and all you need to do is notice this loving guidance.

"You can look to animals for anything and everything that is bothering you. We have lots of guidance and love to share. You can easily feel the love we share all the time, but you might not think to ask us about issues you are facing in life. Try it sometime.

"If you are having a bad day, tell your dog or cat or horse what is going on for you and we will respond through behavior to show you support and wisdom that can help you change your perspective or just simply relax. This is the power of animal love and support. It is there right in front of you each day for the taking.

Open your heart and accept animals as your partners in life."

A Message about Support

Dottie, Hereford Cow
Lorna Dove, Washington

"Generosity. As a cow, I'm here to tell you all that animals are helping you through life. We animals, especially farm animals, are extremely generous in our giving of ourselves to better your human experience. I believe you might take this gift for granted though. Many human beings rush through life and fail to see animals as sentient souls. I ask you to open your heart, open your mind, to the truth that all animals are helping you whether you notice it or not. And this gift of support is our generous gift to all human beings."

A Message about Friendship

Doc, Quarter Horse (In Spirit)
Lorna Dove, Washington

"Friendship warms the heart. Friendship lights up your soul light. Do you marvel when you see different species of animals being friendly with each other? This is our natural state with each other. You can learn from these unusual animal friendships how to be a better friend to other people in your life.

"Set aside your judgments and impulses and just feel the strong connection of love between you and a friend. When you have a true friendship of caring love, you feel more supported in life, and life seems easier. Embrace friendship with others and embrace the love in community."

A Message about Joy

Smoke, Domestic Shorthair
Lorna Dove, Washington

"Joy is something you hold inside you. It isn't something you can look for and find outside of you. You find joy inside when you slow down and focus into your heart. Your heart holds so much wisdom for you. Are you aware that you can tap into your inner wisdom and joy inside your heart? Did you know that this is really your spiritual goal to achieve in this lifetime, the centering of yourself into your heart that is filled with joy? Most people are stuck in their heads with their busy thoughts and never think about their heart wisdom. All animals come straight from the heart in all relationships. In this way we are your teachers, helping you to find your heart wisdom so your life can be more joy-filled and fulfilling."

A Message about Family

Gobble Gobble, Wild Turkeys
Lorna Dove, Washington

"Family. Animals were created as family members. So are you human beings. Some people have big families, some have small, some have family struggles, some have family harmony. It's the same for animals who flock together as a clan or family. Animal families care for each other, love each other unconditionally, support each other, uplift each other. Do you do this in your family? Can you love your family members unconditionally? This is the human challenge in life – to master unconditional love of your family, friends, and community. Animals have already mastered this, so look to us and learn."

A Message about Adventure

Scamp, Billy Goat
Bernie and Chris Creelman, California

"Ahhh, you human beings whom I adore! We Billy Goats model fun and adventure for you. It's time to stop holding yourself back from living life to the fullest, including enjoying some crazy times that make you laugh. You don't have to be so serious all the time! Get out there and live life as the grand adventure it truly is."

A Message about Enjoying Life

Each Spring we have all sizes of goats visiting our drainage canals to eat the weeds growing there to clear the area for fire safety. They love their job!

Pygmy Goat (stock photo)

"I tell you to wake up and enjoy life! If you feel lost, there is always help available, just look around you. Life is for living, not hiding. You are surrounded by love even if you do not feel it. Open your heart to new possibilities and watch your life transform! Bring enjoyment back into your life and start living again."

A Message about Animal Advocacy

I have a herd of black cattle living across the road from me here in Northern California. They seem to live a life of leisure, grazing happily in the sunshine.

Black Cattle (stock photo)

"My name is Bella. I love human beings. Tell humanity to wake up! We animals are not for eating. We are here as companions and guides in life. We are alive, have souls and feel emotions just like you. Please consider eating plant foods and becoming an advocate for all animals on Earth. Thank you!"

Chapter Fourteen - Wisdom of the Wild

The following wild animal wisdom is shared through my own personal encounters with wild animals and an amazing story from my friend Debera A. Butler, Doctor of Veterinarian Medicine. My own personal experiences began back in 2014, when I would speak to wild animals and share their messages via Messages of the Wild on Facebook. I would see interesting wild animal stories in the news and talk to the animal(s) involved to obtain their wisdom. All were delighted to talk!

As Nicholas the Asian Bull Elephant shared with us, wild animals have a global mission to teach humanity lessons about life. Many times, there are unusual circumstances with wild animals, like in Dr. Butler's story. These events always carry an important message from the animal to human beings. For eons of time we human beings have not fully enjoyed the wild animals as they are meant to be known. A few adventurers have paved the way in helping us understand the wild, such as Jane Goodall, Primatologist and Jacque Cousteau,

Ocean Conservationist. Allow the spiritual wisdom of the wild to inspire your perception of life and the connection we all share.

Special Guest
Debera A. Butler, DVM, Arizona
The Tale of the Elk, the Tire Swing, and the Veterinarian

"On Saturday, September 3, 2016, I was standing on my back patio in Pine, Arizona when I saw an Elk walking through my yard. I had to do a double take because I thought my eyes were playing tricks on me! This poor guy had a tire swing completely tangled in his antlers. He had a tire hanging on the right side and a large log hanging on the left side. He was in obvious distress, as the log and tire kept hitting him in the face.

Tire Swing Lucky

"I called multiple agencies/veterinarians and they were either unwilling or unable to help me. After hitting nothing but dead ends, I decided I needed to do something myself. I put corn on my back table and the Elk immediately came up to me before I was done pouring it. This told me he would let me get close to him. My neighbor retrieved his long tree trimmer (which was over six feet long) and he and his son-in-law attempted to cut the rope that the log was hanging from, but as soon as they got near him, he spooked.

"After these failed attempts, everyone left. I sat in my kitchen and started praying that the Elk would understand that I was trying to help him. I stood up and he was back at the table. I grabbed my very old pruners and slowly approached him and kept talking to him to tell him I wanted to help. He let me get near him and I was able to take my first cut of the rope. My pruners were dull, so it took at least six cuts to get through the rope. He would back away after each cut, yet I would encourage him to come back. I finally got the log free, which was bothering him a lot since it was continually banging him in the face.

"I then worked on the tire portion, which was harder since there were two ropes involved and they were touching his face. I was able to get one small cut into one of the ropes before he became exhausted and decided to nap. He laid in my yard for two hours and then returned for more. I tried to cut more of the rope at this time but was only able to get tiny little nips at the rope. He again laid down to rest.

"After more unsuccessful attempts, I decided to go out to dinner. I returned at dusk, which was 12 hours after the Elk had first arrived, to find him at my table again. I noticed that he had successfully rubbed his antlers in the trees enough to break the one rope that I had been working on all day. He actually broke one of my smaller trees in half doing this!

"I asked my brother to hold a flashlight for me as I worked on cutting the final rope. When I saw it was no longer touching his face, I knew I could get it. I slowly walked up to the Elk and told him I could do it if he would remain still for me. I got the rope in two cuts and he was then free from the tire! I jumped up and down with excitement! I couldn't believe I didn't spook him when I was cheering. He ate more corn and then walked away.

"I was later told that while I was at dinner, my neighbor tried again to cut the rope with his tree trimmers, but the elk was scared and wouldn't let him near him. That's when they said I must be "The Elk Whisperer" since I was the only one who could get close to him.

"On Sunday, I did not see the Elk who we named "TS Lucky" (Tire Swing), but he returned on Monday three times. He had removed all of the rope from the right side of his antlers and only had tangled rope remaining on his left side. He eventually got all the rope off and would continue to stop by for an occasional visit. We had such a bond it was so obvious he knew who I was and that I had saved him. I haven't seen him since August of 2017, so I'm guessing a hunter got him.

"I have been criticized by many who either told me I had no business doing what I did since I could have been severely injured or killed and/or I am fooling myself to think that I had a bond with this Elk. All I can say to the critics is, I KNOW we had a special bond, we had looked deep into each other's eyes. He trusted me and I trusted him. If I had to do it all over again, I absolutely would without hesitation. This was a miracle that I will never forget."

***

Dr. Butler's experience is a testament to the animal/human relationship! The Elk instinctively felt her compassion and knew he could trust her. Animals know by feeling when someone is good hearted, or someone intends harm. Debera's kind words, soft voice, and gentle approach showed the Elk she could help him, which created mutual trust. Together they have a family bond that will never be broken, forged through loving kindness. That special bond is real, tangible, and comes from Spirit. This Elk teaches us that mutual respect and kindness are necessary for healthy relationships; and those who care for animals truly have an open heart. Thank you Debera for supporting both pets and wild animals with your deep compassionate spirit.

***

The following messages are from the encounters I have almost daily with wild animals. As an Animal Communicator, animals know who I am by the love and respect I broadcast. Sometimes I feel like I have a neon sign above my head that reads, Animal Communicator. I believe animals know who I am because Spirit guides them. It is funny that if you just say hello to any animal, a powerful conversation can unfold. Most wild animals do not expect to communicate with human beings, so when it happens, they are ecstatic with joy.

A Message about our Ecosystem

On a sunny Sunday morning I was returning to my car after grocery shopping when a Bee landed in my hair. I said hello!

Bee, California (stock photo)

"Hey, BEEutiful being! We Bees partner with you in life to help provide your food. Are you aware of our decline? This is happening because of the horrible pesticides used on plant stock that produces food. Please stop the madness! You live in a Holy ecosystem where all things work together for the good of all. Those evil chemicals destroy the balance, and we Bees suffer. Yes, we are an insect, but all insects play an important part in our ecosystem of life. Please open your heart to understanding the importance of insects, let go of your fear, grow food organically, and let us do our job. Human beings cannot control nature; chemicals destroy it. It is now time for you to save us, for when you take care of us you take care of yourself, your family and the world!"

A Message about Divine Connection

The month of April brought hundreds of butterflies each day flying West in my hometown. They would flutter around cars while driving, a magical experience. I asked them why they were all flying West.

Butterflies during Migration in California (stock photo)

"We butterflies on the move send a message to all humans who delight in us - It's time for you to take flight and find your way back to the Creator's love! Stop goofing around trying to handle everything yourself. There is powerful help available to you. As we surround you, so does divine love surround you. We embrace you with this love so pause and feel it! A butterfly's wings spread love everywhere. Why do we fly West? We are butterflies in migration, and so are you! Have you ever noticed that life never stands still, it is always in motion in a forward movement for positive change. Embrace your life's journey as it unfolds before you knowing you are led by love."

A Message about Upliftment

I was out walking one day and encountered two turkey vultures flying high over a canal near my home. This was the first time I ever saw them in a residential neighborhood, a true surprise! Their wingspan is magnificent.

Turkey Vulture, California (stock photo)

"Human beings are meant to soar above their troubles in life. We know it is hard when you get stuck in your heavy emotions. When you are in a time of worry or struggle, step outside and watch the birds. Allow the birds to lift your spirit on their wings, give your troubles to our Great Spirit and let the birds carry them away so you can feel better inside. Nature and wild animals are here to uplift you and support you in life if you will open your heart and mind to our support."

A Message about the Outdoors

Laura lives on a ranch in Colorado where many wild animals stop by to visit. She enjoys her wild animal encounters and embraces all animals with love. Here a pregnant Moose shares her wisdom.

Moose, Colorado
Photo Courtesy of Laura Summers

"My advice to you is to get outdoors more! You underestimate the power of Nature. Human beings have become so sedentary, and that is not good for you. Put aside your electronic devices, step outside and breath in the fresh air. It does a body good, and a soul too. You are made to be outdoors, enjoying the weather in all its seasons, breathing clean air, having fun in the sun. We wild animals model this for you. Step outside, breathe, relax, and let go of things you don't need, feeling your connection to all of life!"

A Message about Exploration

I was reading an online newspaper and saw a news story of a rare sighting of a Gannet flying around Alcatraz Island in San Francisco. Had a lovely chat!

Gannet on Alcatraz Island, California (stock photo)

"Get out and explore the world! You have a new world filled with love and light. Seek the beauty in life and soar high above the perceived chaos."

A Message about Relationship

Wild Horse, Colorado
Photo Courtesy of Catherine Michaels

"Relationship is everything. You humans do not seem to understand the connection we share together as sentient souls. Some people think they can control wild animals and even nature herself. Ha! It is very foolish of your big egos to believe that. Only the one true God is in control of this entire world, not you! I know that those of you reading this are animal lovers, so I do apologize for my ranting against those who don't really care about animals or this world. I appreciate your support in helping wild horses to stay free to roam the countryside where we belong."

A Message about Racism

This message is from a news story of a white deer sighted in San Francisco darting across a field near the Golden Gate Bridge, an unusual sight that snarled traffic.

White Albino Deer, California (stock photo)

"You notice me because I am white, a different color from my family. Yet am I not still a deer? Am I not still the same as my family, except for my outside color? Yes, I am the same on the inside as all other deer. The racism in human society is a lie when spoken. You are different colors on the outside but the same on the inside. Please realize this truth and end racism."

A Message about the Wild

A Mountain Lion was seen walking in a residential neighborhood of Sacramento, California, unnerving the residents there.

Mountain Lion (stock photo)

"People, listen to the call of the wild. We are your guiding light. Treat us with respect and kindness, for when you do this you open your heart to new possibilities."

A Message about Connection

Sparrows abound in California and are a common backyard visitor at our home.

Sparrow, California (stock photo)

"We see so many humans who feel alone and misunderstood. Do not feel lonely. You are surrounded by love. Just step outside. You can talk to us, not just us birds, but all of life."

A Message about Fear

A message from a bird who visited my backyard.

Black Phoebe, California (stock photo)

"Many of you have lived with fear for so long that you are not aware of how it controls you. Many of you are forgetting that the Earth provides all that you need. Most of your fears arise from things you imagine will happen but rarely do. Leave behind your fears and be free. You were born to be free and to love."

A Message about Joy

Hummingbirds are a part of my backyard wildlife. We have a feeder to support them, and they support us with beauty and joy.

Hummingbird, California (stock photo)

"Hummingbirds' message is that of joy. It's time to be carefree in life, let go of worries, live in the beauty of Earth. We are all connected, so talk to us! We make nests where we feel safe. I took up residence in Suzanne's redwood tree named Rob. She is enjoying watching me sit, beholding the beautiful nest I built. I chose her home because I could feel the love and I was attracted to it. I invite you, as does the entire Animal Kingdom, to partner with us to heal this world. We are all connected by love. Open your hearts to the wonders of life that surround you. Life is amazing!"

A Message about Freedom

I spoke to this Chameleon in our local pet store, who asked me to share this message.

Chameleon, California

"Animals of the wild are not meant to be your pet. While some wild souls choose to become a pet for the life experience, some do not. I am one who has chosen to experience a human relationship to better understand human beings. It was my soul choice. I speak on behalf of those captured from the wild to become pets. Leave them to be free!"

A Message about Timing

This peacock stood in front of a door I was attempting to go through at an office complex, so I asked if it had a message to share. That day I was struggling with self-doubt about my purpose.

Peacock, California

"You are always in the right place at the right time. So many of you assume you know what your life is about. Everyday though there are signs all around you for you to see and take in to help lead you in life. We wild animals are one of those signs. We carry messages of love and hope for you. When you have an animal encounter you are in the right place at the right time. Take notice, get curious, and listen. Then trust that you are being led by the highest love in the Universe – the Holy Spirit. That love will always lead you in the right direction. It is your job to learn to trust that leadership."

A Message about Listening

I arrived at work early in the morning. As I parked my car, three black crows where shouting excitedly at me.

Black Crows, California (stock photo)

"Ha! Yes, we do have a message that can change your life! You silly human beings run around all stuck in your head – meaning nonstop thoughts swirling around and around like a crazy circus. When you hear a Crow's calling, listen! We are literally calling you out of your mental-ness and into your heart! We do this to assist you in understanding and focusing more on all of life, your connection to life, the importance of life and connection to Spirit. You are NOT your mind; you are your heart.

"Listen to our calls to you and don't be annoyed (we are loud for a reason!). Know that we support your life!!! All bird vocalizations do this. So next time you hear any bird singing, listen and enjoy the loving support provided."

A Message about Remorse

We have wild turkeys that forage everywhere in our town. This turkey was in the parking lot of our local movie theater when we had our conversation.

City Turkey, California

"Remorse is something that you human beings might be carrying around. I feel it a lot in people who pass by in their cars or walking down the street. Although they never stop to say hello, I always say hello and can feel their unhappiness. Remorse isn't something you need to carry around like baggage through your lifetime – you can choose to change! You can choose to heal! You can choose a different healthy perspective! Instead of being remorseful, get outside and say hello to a wild animal and feel the love we wish to share with you and smile."

Effie Yeaw Nature Center, California

I visited Effie Yeaw Sacramento Nature Center with my friend Norma and a group of animal lovers to do some hiking. This beautiful park is filled with wildlife to behold. We saw bucks and does, turkeys, turkey vultures, woodpeckers, and many other birds. We saw a baby hawk high up in a tree, sitting outside the nest on a branch so I spoke to him. We also encountered a squirrel who had a message to share. The whole park is teaming with good vibes alongside the Sacramento River. I had the pleasure of meeting Orion, a young Swainson's Hawk, and two other animals.

A Message about Supporting Animals

Orion, Swainson's Hawk

"I am an ambassador bird here to teach people to love and care for animals. Humans rescued me and helped me to heal. Now I return this gift to all humanity. I say to you Wake Up! Start helping all animals, even the tiny insect. Partner with animals in your life. Shake off personal lies and live your truth. Most of all be kind to every animal you encounter."

A Message about Family

Wild Baby Hawk, Effie Yeaw Nature Preserve
Photo courtesy of Catherine Moody

"I share a message about family. Family is so important to your happiness. If you feel like you don't belong, then seek the outdoor family that surrounds you with love. Step outside and say hello! We consider you a part of our family."

A Message about Having Fun

Wild Squirrel, Effie Yeaw Nature Preserve
Photo courtesy of Crystal Connor

"I'm watching you! Thank you for loving animals so much. I just love seeing visitors who care. We squirrels represent fun, and I hope you are having fun today as you stroll through the park. I wish you glad tidings and joy!"

A Message about Peace

There has been a recent resurgence of Humpback Whales in Northern California reported in the news. I had the pleasure of talking to one of these magnificent creatures.

Humpback Whale in San Francisco Bay (stock photo)

"Whales represent BIG peace and easy flow. We model this for you by gliding through the ocean but also jumping for joy. This is how life should be for all, free flowing and at times very joyful. Whales also anchor God's love into the waterways of Earth. Swimming in pods we can generate huge amounts of love that benefits everyone. Say hello the next time you see us, we love you!"

Chapter Fifteen - Animal Conservation

Nola the Northern White Rhinoceros, formerly of San Diego Safari Park (In spirit)

I met Nola during a visit to the San Diego Safari Park with my husband in August of 2015. Three months later she passed. At that time, Nola was one of only four Northern White Rhinos left in the world, according to the Park. As of 2019, only two male white rhinos remain in the Ol Pejeta Conservancy in Kenya under 24-hour armed guard. My heart breaks knowing we human beings have destroyed this species. May Nola's wisdom touch your heart.

"I love all human beings. While at the safari park they took such good care of me. My handlers always knew what I wanted or needed. I am grateful for their care. Human beings have destroyed our species! I am angry about that but understand human ignorance. It is time for people to wake up and end the killing of all animals, both domesticated and wild.

"Animals have a soul, just like you. We have feelings and emotions, just like you. We are your partners in life, not a lesser species. Please open your hearts and see the truth of who animals are – living beings with a soul just like you. When people hurt animals, they hurt themselves. There is human evil in this world that must be eradicated!

"My species will go extinct in YOUR LIFETIME! You can end extinction on Earth by simply taking action to end it. Do not sit idly by, step forward and care. **Nothing changes unless people demand change and take action.** Peace starts in your own heart, so do the inner work to heal yourself, then work on healing this planet. YOU can do it; you must do it! Do not wait for others to take action - you take action and fulfill your part in making this world a better place.

"God bless all those who care for the Animal Kingdom. My species will not survive because of human evil. Make this the last time, please! End hunting for sport and egotistical pride, end killing for animal parts that do not heal humans. Start revering and respecting all animals as sentient souls. We are a team, you and I, and working together we can change this world. I ask YOU, in the name of the Holy Spirit, to bring positive change to this world."

When I first met Nola I could feel her inner grief of knowing she was the last female Northern White Rhino on Earth. I could not even imagine her pain and apologized on behalf of all human beings. I hid my tears behind sunglasses so others would not notice. Now I wish I hadn't. In hiding my tears, I was being one of those human beings not speaking out in defense of animals. I allowed my personal fear of embarrassment hold me back. No more!

Animal advocacy is everyone's job, including my own. If you are an animal lover think about what you can do to support wild animals and end extinction on Earth. Speak up! Let your compassion and Spirit's love lead the way. Our world depends on it. My wish is for the end of all wild animal capture, enslavement, and abuse to perform or become a 'pet'; stop the needless hunting and slaughter for human greed. May Spirit cleanse the human evil from this world for the wellbeing of animals everywhere and the survival of all species.

What can you do? Support legislation that is trying to end animal abuse of both pets and wild animals. Be a voice for the animals. Become a member of your favorite shelter, animal advocacy organization or sanctuary and support them through donations or volunteer work. I like the work of the World Wildlife Fund for their conservation efforts worldwide to protect the future of wild animals and nature.

Most importantly, visit captive animals in pet stores, shelters, zoos, and sanctuaries and tell them through love how much you respect and honor them. It can be that simple – just spread your compassionate love to animals so they can forgive us and heal. It all begins with taking the first step in becoming a partner in conservation.

"A dream remains a dream without action upon it."

Jack, Tabby Cat

Chapter Sixteen - The Snow White Life

For years my life has been filled with all manner of wild animal encounters . It occurs all the time, everywhere I go. I do not seek these encounters, they happen naturally. When they happen, it makes me take notice and ask, what are these animals trying to tell me? Wild animals have shared both messages for humanity and messages that support my own life.

I've had a mama hummingbird take up residence in a redwood tree in our backyard. Her name was Lita. I introduced myself and she giggled saying, "Woo hoo, we bring you joy!" Delightful!

One night I was standing outside in downtown Sacramento chatting with friends when a raccoon causally walked down the sidewalk. It glanced at us, saying "Hello" and kept going. It is comical to see a raccoon in the downtown area! I got in my car to leave and as I pulled out of the driveway, two raccoons were walking the other direction on the sidewalk. I guess the first raccoon found his friend. Raccoon's message to me was "transformation is in the air."

The next morning, I was standing in the kitchen and a

spider scurried across on the floor yelling, "Look out, coming through!" I laughed! Spider's message was, "Keep moving forward no matter how big the obstacles seem." Ok.

Pondering all these encounters, I went out in the back yard. There was a dove flying around cooing. She landed on a redwood tree branch. I introduced myself and welcomed her to our home. She giggled. I think there may be a nest on that branch. Doves represent peace...So what were all these animal encounters trying to tell me?

LIFE IS MAGICAL!
Hi ho, hi ho...

When you walk through life attuned to all of life you can experience the magic around you. Life becomes magical, mystical, wonderous, and exciting. I never feel alone, always noticing what's happening around me, understanding I am a small part of this cosmic mix of life with all living beings. It is a feeling of connection, belonging, and support. This amazes me to know that wild animals support human life so much.

Animals understand human beings better than we understand ourselves. This is not by accident; it is by divine design. One day I was feeling very down, sitting at my kitchen table moping. Suddenly a Praying Mantis landed on my sliding glass door. It was huge! It grabbed my attention and before I could say anything it began talking to me. "Why are you sad? You are a beautiful woman with so much to give this world. Cheer up and see how important you are." The mantis brought tears to my eyes, and I was a bit surprised an insect would counsel me that way. When things like that happen, if you listen it can change your entire perspective.

Knowing that animals speak through spirit means I listen every time one talks because I hear the voice of Spirit talking. The Holy Spirit speaks in many different ways through animals. The next time your cat jumps in your lap, think about the Spirit connection and wonder. Gaze into the eyes of your beloved pet and see the unconditional love emanating from your pet and our Creator. It is a depth of Spirit that abounds in animals for our greater good.

Take a walk outside and notice who you encounter. Hear the chatter of birds, feel the breeze on your face, the warmth of the sun upon your skin. Set the intention to connect with all of life and experience the magical side of life with animals as your guide. Even the plants and trees are talking, if you are willing to listen and whistle while you work.

Willow Tree in San Diego, California

It is inspiring to notice the deep connections we have with all of life. This magic happened when I arrived at my hotel room at the Paradise Point Resort in San Diego. The patio overlooked a small pond with a lovely weeping willow tree. I felt drawn to this tree and asked if I could speak to her. She agreed, so I introduced myself and learned her name was Myla. As we talked, I could feel her deep love for this world. An old wise soul, Myla delivered a message.

Wise Willow Tree

"We are all connected to each other and our ancestors. This is why our world is currently rumbling with pain from the past. You know of what I speak – racism, bigotry, hatred, oppression, all deeply woven into the web of life on Earth.

"It falls on your shoulders to make new choices in order to heal the pain of the past. How? When you face a situation of hatred, make a choice to confront it peacefully, not feeding into the pain with more hatred. If you think hateful thoughts, recognize those thoughts and reframe them into positive ones.

"In order for this world to become more peaceful YOU must be that inside yourself. When you can finally achieve this new way of being alive, the world shifts, changes and heals along with you.

"Stop and realize your life is powerful! Look inside, love yourself and that inner love will expand outward into the world, healing the world. Love is the most important feeling of all and you hold this inside yourself. Love is all we are."

Her wisdom brought tears to my eyes. My connection with this tree soul was just like my human and animal connections. Those connections are through love, in human beings, in animals, in water, in air, in Earth. Her words are profound, and I have taken heed in my own life with this message of love.

Every living thing on Earth has a soul with wisdom to share. Human beings can be naïve and even ignorant to the life around them. As a species, we humans are no better than any animal, any tree, any other living being, yet we seem to want to place ourselves above them through our egotistical behaviors. A better way is to cultivate respect for every living being. This allows unconditional love to take root and spread outward for the benefit of everyone.

"Only you can change your life."

Oliver, Lab

About the Author

Honored to be an Animal Communicator and Advocate for this beautiful Earth, Suzanne Thibault supports animal lovers to communicate effectively with animals for a magical life. It is the animals in her life that have helped her awaken to the deep spiritual connection we all share as sentient souls through the mighty love of the Holy Spirit.

As a Spiritual Life Coach, her passion is to support the end of suffering for both people and animals for a peaceful, happy life. Her own personal healing journey of childhood emotional pain began her animal communication abilities. All the animals throughout her life have guided her way and taught her what needed healing for spiritual growth.

Suzanne takes a stand for her client's personal and spiritual growth, supporting both women and animals to embrace their life's potential through the foundation of emotional heart healing that dramatically improves their life. She inspires and challenges women to deepen their relationship with animals and Spirit for their self-care. Through divine inner healing, Suzanne shines the light on emotional pain that leads to healing as they make peace with the past.

Her core message, that **Love Makes All Things Possible**, was born from her childhood dog Wiggles saving her life as a young child in a highly dysfunctional family. She learned then about the animal/human bond of unconditional love that is so strong it saves your life, and now shares this wisdom with animal lovers everywhere.

As the podcast host of Spiritual Straight Talk, Suzanne and her guests inspire you to deepen your self-care in life and business. As the founder of Suzanne Thibault Academy, she provides animal communication and divine inner healing training programs.

As a Premier Member of the Women Speakers Association, Suzanne speaks straight from the heart to inspire spiritually aligned women to embrace their pet's support. Audiences find her innovative work life-changing with easy to understand concepts for quick implementation. Suzanne's inspirational approach fast-tracks audiences towards succeeding in making a deeper connection to inner wisdom and animal communication, which empowers and enriches their life.

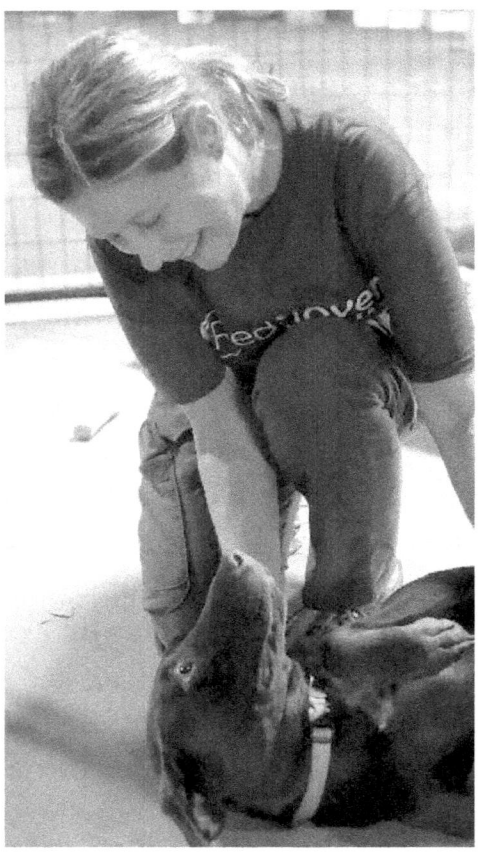

Caring for Dixie Lou

Suzanne's volunteer work as a Red Rover Responder, supports animals in crisis to bring them emotional peace and divine healing for a better life. Her philanthropic work is her way of giving back for all she has received from Spirit and her animal family.

Recommended Resources

To learn more about Suzanne Thibault:
  https://www.suzannethibault.net
  https://suzanne-thibault-academy.thinkific.com/

For a free copy of *The Fur Agreements,* by Dr. Tricia Working:
  https://www.pawsforthoughtinc.com

Effie Yeaw Nature Center, California
  https://www.sacnaturecenter.net/

Performing Animal Welfare Society (PAWS)
  https://www.pawsweb.org/

Red Rover, Bringing Animals from Crisis to Care
  https://redrover.org/

San Diego Safari Park
  https://www.sdzsafaripark.org/

World Wildlife Fund for Conservation
  https://www.worldwildlife.org/

In Gratitude

To Angela Kindley Dennis and her pets Henri, Kaylee and Freya, for providing the love-filled cover photo for this book, thank you! Angela is a professional photographer, animal advocate and pet mom to her large animal family. Contact her at angela@alphadogcreative.com.

Learn more at alphadogcreative.com.

To Norma Springsteen, for providing in-depth editing for this book, thank you! Norma is multi-talented on a professional administrative level plus is passionate about energy healing and nature. Connect with Norma at nyspingsteen@gmail.com.

Learn more at
https://nyspringsteen.wixsite.com/openheart.

www.ingramcontent.com/pod-product-compliance
Lightning Source LLC
Chambersburg PA
CBHW052026070526
44584CB00016B/1923